Headway

Academic Skills

Listening, Speaking, and Study Skills

LEVEL 3 **Teacher's Guide**

Sue Hobbs
Series Editors: Liz and John Soars

OXFORD

Great Clarendon Street, Oxford, OX2 6DP, United Kingdom

Oxford University Press is a department of the University of Oxford.
It furthers the University's objective of excellence in research, scholarship,
and education by publishing worldwide. Oxford is a registered trade
mark of Oxford University Press in the UK and in certain other countries

ISBN: 978 0 19 474212 2   Book
ISBN: 978 0 19 474167 5   Pack
ISBN: 978 0 19 474205 4   Test CD-ROM

Printed in Spain by Unigraf S.L.

This book is printed on paper from certified and well-managed sources

ACKNOWLEDGEMENTS

*Although every effort has been made to trace and contact copyright holders before
publication, this has not been possible in some cases. We apologise for any apparent
infringement of copyright and, if notified, the publisher will be pleased to rectify any
errors or omissions at the earliest possible opportunity.*

Contents

Introduction

Headway Academic Skills

Headway Academic Skills is a multi-level course aimed at post-secondary students who need English in their academic studies. It comprises a Student's Book and Teacher's Guide for each strand and each level.

Each level consists of 10 units covering a variety of topics relevant to students in higher education. Units focus on a wide range of academic listening, speaking, research, and/or vocabulary skills.

Headway Academic Skills can be used alongside *New Headway* and *New Headway Plus*, or alongside any other general English course.

Aims of *Headway Academic Skills*

The aims of *Headway Academic Skills* are to help post-secondary students become more efficient and effective in their studies by:

- developing strategies to improve listening skills, and to build up the techniques required for academic study, including note-taking in lectures, and developing critical thinking;
- developing strategies to improve speaking skills, and to build confidence in expressing ideas and opinions, and giving presentations;
- encouraging them to adopt various approaches for dealing with new or unknown vocabulary by practising effective use of dictionaries, and through making effective vocabulary records;
- exploring and evaluating research techniques and resources, and crediting sources of information;
- promoting learner independence by encouraging students to return to earlier Study Skills to refresh their memories, or to see how new skills build on and develop those previously presented.

Students are given opportunities to practise their listening and speaking skills through brainstorming sessions, discussing issues, and sharing thoughts in realistic academic situations.

Ultimately, *Headway Academic Skills* also aims to develop academic skills by being transferable to all areas of students' day-to-day academic studies.

What's in the Student's Books?

Each unit of *Headway Academic Skills LEVEL 3* consists of 7–8 hours of lessons. There are four or five sections in each unit, which include Listening, Speaking, Vocabulary Development, and Review. A Research section also appears in three units. Each Listening, Speaking, Vocabulary Development, and Research section has clear study skill aims presented in Study Skill boxes. These skills are practised through a series of controlled to freer practice exercises.

Language Bank boxes highlight the functional language which students may need to complete the speaking task.

LISTENING

Each listening section contains one or more listenings which students use to develop different study skills. These study skills are clearly detailed in Study Skill boxes and are linked to specific practice exercises. The listenings are of various types and styles which students will come across during the course of their academic studies, including lectures, discussions, seminars, and academic podcasts.

SPEAKING

Each speaking section has clear outcomes for the students in terms of the type of task they may be asked to perform, including summaries, discussions, and presentations using visual prompts. The skills covered take the students through the speaking process from brainstorming ideas, making notes, selecting and organizing notes, composing effective introductions and conclusions, and giving full presentations.

VOCABULARY DEVELOPMENT

The vocabulary section contains skills and strategies which help students develop good vocabulary learning and recording techniques. It encourages them to become more autonomous learners by making them more effective users of dictionaries, helping them to work out meanings of new words, and encouraging them to keep coherent and well-organized vocabulary records.

RESEARCH

The principal skills addressed in this section are formulating efficient research plans, and finding and assessing reliable sources of information such as an encyclopaedia and the Internet. This section also deals with the importance of recording and crediting sources which students use in their academic work.

REVIEW

In the review section, students are given the opportunity to reflect on skills learnt, to practise and develop them further, and to consider how these could be applied to their academic studies.

AUDIO SCRIPT

There is a complete audio script in the back of the Student's Book.

IELTS and TOEFL

Whilst this course does not deal specifically with the questions which occur in public examinations such as IELTS and TOEFL, many of the skills taught in this course have a direct application to preparing for these exams.

Headway Academic Skills Teacher's Guide

The Teacher's Guide is an easy-to-follow resource for the teacher offering step-by-step guidance to teaching *Headway Academic Skills*. As well as step-by-step procedural notes, the Teacher's Guide contains a summary of aims, lead-in tasks, background information, extension activities, and a comprehensive answer key.

Why use a Teacher's Guide?

Both the Teacher's Guides and the Student's Books have been very carefully devised in order to develop specific academic skills. As such, the treatment of materials is often different from that in a general English course. For example, pre-teaching difficult vocabulary from a text before the students read it may interfere with subsequent skills work on drawing meaning from context, or on extracting only the essential information from a complex text. Teachers are therefore strongly encouraged to consult the Teacher's Guide.

What's in the Teacher's Guide?

AIMS

Each listening, speaking, vocabulary development, research, and review section has a summary of the aims of that section.

LEAD IN

Lead-in activities are devised to focus students' attention on the topic and skills of each section.

PROCEDURE

Class management and step-by-step instructions.

EXTENSION ACTIVITIES

Extension activities offer ideas on how to extend skills practice, or give students an opportunity to reflect on their learning.

ADDITIONAL PHOTOCOPIABLE ACTIVITY

There is one extra practice activity for each unit with step-by-step instructions at the back of the Teacher's Guide.

ANSWER KEY

For ease of use, the answer key is on the same page as the teaching notes for each exercise, but presented separately. The answer key for each exercise is clearly referenced in the procedural notes. For example, exercise 1 key is referenced ⊶1.

AUDIO SCRIPT

There is a complete audio script on pp57–76 of the Teacher's Guide.

Class Audio CDs

The audio to accompany the Student's Book is available on Class Audio CDs. It is intended that these will be used by the teacher in class.

Selected audio from the Review sections is also available online at:
www.oup.com/elt/headway/audio
This can be used by students for homework or self-study.

We hope you and your students enjoy working with Headway Academic Skills.

1 Learning and intelligence

LISTENING SKILLS Listening for gist • Listening for specific information • Critical thinking (1) Defining terms • Understanding the language of graphs

SPEAKING SKILLS Assessing yourself • Taking turns in a discussion

VOCABULARY DEVELOPMENT Knowing a word

LISTENING How to be a successful student pp4–5

AIMS

The aims of this section are to help students listen for gist and for specific information. Additional aims are to develop critical thinking skills and to help students understand the language of graphs.

LEAD IN

- Focus the students' attention on the page. Ask them to identify the skill LISTENING, and the topic (*How to be a successful student*).
- Tell students to look at the photo. Ask them to suggest reasons why students decide to go to university (*to get a good career, to make their family proud, because they enjoy studying, to become independent*).

PROCEDURE

1 Students read the instructions and discuss the questions in groups. Ask them to write their ideas in the table. Go round and monitor. Get feedback from the whole class. **⊶ 1**

2 ◉ **1.1** Students read the **STUDY SKILL** and the instructions, and then read the general points. Point out that they won't be listening for detailed information. Play the CD.

3 ◉ **1.1** Students compare their answers in pairs then listen again to check their answers. Explain the answers as a class, if necessary. **⊶ 3**

4 ◉ **1.2** Students read the **STUDY SKILL** and the instructions. Elicit that they'll be listening to the second part of the talk and that they need to record specific information in column A of the table. Students listen to the CD and complete the task. **⊶ 4**

5 ◉ **1.2** Focus their attention again on the Study Skill. Students listen to the CD again and complete column B with the signalling phrases. Check answers with the whole class. **⊶ 5**

LISTENING Answer key pp4–5

⊶ 1

Possible answers
1 Successful students are motivated, organize their resources, work well with others, and know their strengths and weaknesses.
2 Unsuccessful students are lazy, don't organize their notes, don't read and listen carefully, and don't ask tutors and lecturers for advice.

⊶ 3

2 and 5.

⊶ 4

A advice
- time management
- meet deadlines
- organize the resources you need
- find out which people are available
- find out your strengths and weaknesses

⊶ 5

B language signals
- One of the most important skills is …
- Following on from that – another piece of advice …
- The next bit of advice concerns …
- Another important resource is …
- The final point is …

Intelligence and learning pp5–7

1 Students read the instructions and do the quiz. 🔑 1

2 Students read the instructions and discuss their results in pairs. Elicit ideas from some students.

3 Students read the **STUDY SKILL**. Ask them to discuss the questions in small groups. Have a class discussion based upon their responses.

4 Students read the instructions and the definitions, and tick their choices. Get feedback from the class.

5 Students write their own definitions. Go round and monitor. Elicit some definitions and give feedback.

6 Students read the instructions and decide whether the statements are True or False. Check the answers as a class. 🔑 6

7 💿 **1.3** Students read the **STUDY SKILL** and the instructions. Play the CD. Check the answer as a class. 🔑 7

8 💿 **1.4** Students read the instructions, listen to the CD, and do the task. Check the answers as a class. 🔑 8

9 💿 **1.5** Students read the instructions and complete the handout. Elicit the answers from some students. 🔑 9

EXTENSION ACTIVITY

Play 💿 **1.4** again. Ask the students to focus on signalling words and phrases and write the ones used by the speaker. You could point out that some phrases are used specifically to sequence and others to signal explanations. Then put the students into pairs or small groups to compare notes.

LISTENING Answer key pp5–7

🔑 1

1 12.

2

3 False.

🔑 6

1 F 2 T 3 F 4 T

🔑 7

Graph b.

🔑 8

1 c 2 g 3 a 4 b 5 f 6 d 7 e

🔑 9

1 For education and society:
Schools focus most attention on **just two types (linguistic and logical-mathematical).**
But schools should also focus on **the other intelligences.**
2 For teachers:
Teachers should **teach in a variety of ways.**

SPEAKING Assessing study habits p8

AIMS

The aims of this section are to help students assess and describe their strengths, weaknesses and habits, and to practise taking turns in a discussion.

LEAD IN

- Ask the students to think of someone they know well who has a particular skill or strength. Put students in pairs and ask them to tell their partner about the person and what they're good at. Tell them to ask each other questions to get as much information as possible. Go round and monitor.
- Invite some students to tell the whole class about the people they chose.

PROCEDURE

1 Students read the **STUDY SKILL** and list their strengths and weaknesses.

2 Students read the instructions and answer the questions.

3 🔘 **1.6** Students read the instructions. Play the CD. Students complete the table. Check the answers as a class. **⚬┐ 3**

4 Put the students in pairs or small groups. Focus their attention on the expressions in the Language Bank. Students discuss their strengths, weaknesses and study habits. Monitor and encourage discussion where necessary.

Taking part in a discussion p9

1 Students read the instructions and do the task.

2 Ask students to compare their results in pairs. Encourage them to explain their choices. Go round and monitor.

3 🔘 **1.7** Students read the **STUDY SKILL** and the instructions. Focus their attention on the expressions in the Language Bank. Students listen to the CD and complete the box. Check the examples together. **⚬┐ 3**

4 Students study the discussion questions and make notes. Explain that this is preparation for a discussion on the topic.

5 Focus the students' attention on the Language Bank expressions and then ask them to read the instructions. Point out the three aspects of this task. Put the students into groups of three or four and ask them to discuss the questions in exercise 4.

6 Have a group feedback session which covers the views of each group and also their assessment of how the discussion went.

ADDITIONAL PHOTOCOPIABLE ACTIVITY

Speaking 1 Group discussion

EXTENSION ACTIVITY

Students listen to 🔘 **1.7** again and read the audio script on p58. Put them in small groups. Ask them to discuss the possible body language of the speakers at different points in the dialogue, particularly thinking about how we use our hands to politely indicate handing over, taking the floor, or holding the floor. Discuss as a class.

SPEAKING Answer key p8

⚬┐ 3

Sarah
Weaknesses: <u>leaves revision to the last minute</u>
Strengths: <u>performs well in seminar discussions</u>
Time of study: <u>in the evenings after lectures</u>
Place of study: <u>in the library</u>
Takes breaks? <u>yes, usually takes one every hour</u>
Takes notes? <u>yes, a lot</u>
Has a study plan? <u>no</u>
Works alone or in groups? <u>prefers to work alone</u>

Andrew
Weaknesses: <u>can't meet deadlines, late with assignments</u>
Strengths: <u>good at making presentations, enjoys talking to people</u>
Time of study: <u>likes the mornings, before breakfast</u>
Place of study: <u>at home in his room</u>
Takes breaks? <u>yes, when he wants</u>
Takes notes? <u>no</u>
Has a study plan? <u>no</u>
Works alone or in groups? <u>belongs to a study group</u>

SPEAKING Answer key p9

⚬┐ 3

Handing over to other people
What do you think?
Don't you agree?

Interrupting
Yes, but ...
I'd like to make a point here.

Holding the floor
Could I just finish?
Well, let me explain.

AIMS

The aim of this section is to help students understand the different aspects of knowing a word and how to find this information in a dictionary.

LEAD IN

- Ask the students to think about the dictionaries they possess (monolingual, bilingual, size, level, etc.). Put them in pairs and tell them to find out which dictionaries their partner owns, how often they use them, and what they use them for.
- Invite some students to feed back to the class. Ask:
  – *Do you think you're using your dictionary in the best possible way?*
  Elicit responses.

PROCEDURE

1 Students read the **STUDY SKILL** and the instructions, and complete the table. Draw the table on the board and check the answers with the whole class. **○┐1**

2 Students read the instructions and complete the task for the word they have chosen, using their dictionaries. Group students who have selected the same word and ask them to check their answers. Assist any individuals. **○┐2**

3 Students read the instructions. Check they understand that the circles indicate the stress pattern of the word. Model the pronunciation. Students use their dictionaries and complete the table with the stress patterns. Write the answers on the board. **○┐3**

4 Students read the instructions and find the parts of speech. Elicit the answers. **○┐4**

5 Students read the instructions and complete the sentences. Elicit answers from the students. **○┐5**

EXTENSION ACTIVITY

Ask the students to look again at the table in exercise 1. Tell them to use a dictionary to look up the forms of the word they chose, and write down the parts of speech and word stress patterns for each form.

Put students back in their groups from exercise 2 above so they can compare the information they find.

Answers

organize (vb), organization (n), organized (adj), organizer (n), organizational (adj)

success (n), successful (adj), succeed (vb), successfully (adv)

logical (adj), logic (n), logically (adv), logician (n)

critical (adj), critic (n), criticism (n), criticize (vb), critique (vb/n), critically (adv)

○┐1

part of speech: adj
pronunciation: /ɪnˈtelɪdʒənt/

○┐2

	organize	success
the meaning	to arrange for something to happen/ to put something in order	the fact that you have achieved something that you want
part of speech	verb	noun
pronunciation	/ˈɔːgənaɪz/	/səkˈses/
synonyms	to plan, structure, order, arrange	achievement
antonyms	–	failure
collocations	something, yourself, somebody, people	have, be a, meet with, make a success of, the key to, sweet, a roaring
forms of the word	organized, organizer, organization, organizational, disorganized	succeed, successful, successfully, unsuccessful

	logical	critical
the meaning	seeming natural, reasonable, or sensible, following the rules of logic	expressing disapproval, making careful judgements about something
part of speech	adj	adj
pronunciation	/ˈlɒdʒɪkl/	/ˈkrɪtɪkl/
synonyms	sensible, rational, reasonable	disapproving, crucial, essential, serious
antonyms	illogical	uncritical
collocations	conclusion, argument, mind	report, comment, acclaim, importance, factor, moment, very, in a critical condition
forms of the word	logic, logically, logician, illogical	critic, critically, criticize, criticism, critique

○┐3

word	stress
intellect	O o o
intelligent	o O o o
intelligently	o O o o o
intelligible	o O o o o

○┐4

intelligence **(n)**
intelligently **(adv)**
intellect **(n)**
intellectual **(adj)**
intelligible **(adj)**

○┐5

1 intelligible
2 intelligently
3 intelligence
4 intelligent
5 intelligence/intellect
6 intellect

REVIEW p11

AIMS

The aims of this section are to give students further practice in the skills learnt in this unit, and to give them the opportunity to review the work they have done. A further aim is to encourage students to apply what they have learnt to their other academic studies in English.

PROCEDURE

1 🔊 **1.8** Students read the instructions. Revise the meanings of 'listening for gist' and 'listening for specific information', if necessary. Play the CD. Students answer the question about the sentences. Check the answers with the class. 🔑 **1**

2 🔊 **1.8** Students read the instructions. Play the CD again. Put students into pairs to check their answers. Monitor and check the answers as a class if necessary. 🔑 **2**

3 🔊 **1.9** Students read the instructions. Play the CD. Students complete the task. Draw the basic graph on the board and ask students to come and label it. 🔑 **3**

4 Students read the instructions and complete the task. Ask them to check their answers with a partner. 🔑 **4**

5 Put the students in groups of three or four. Students read the instructions and complete the task. After the task, refer them back to the Language Bank on p9. Ask:
– *Did you use these expressions in your discussions?*

EXTENSION ACTIVITY

Ask the students to list the skills they have learnt and practised in this unit. For example,
– listening for gist
– listening for specific information
– developing critical thinking skills
– practising taking turns in a discussion
– using a dictionary
Put students in groups to discuss how to apply these skills to the work they do in their academic studies.

REVIEW Answer key p11

🔑 1
1 specific
2 gist
3 specific
4 specific
5 gist

🔑 2
1 She's just started her second year at university.
2 She's studying Engineering.
3 She's got to hand in a research paper on Friday.
4 She tries to start assignments well in advance of the deadlines.

🔑 3
1 1995
2 2000
3 2007

🔑 4
1 Well, not entirely.
2 I'd like to add something here.
3 Could you hold on until I finish, please?
4 Thank you, Tom. I think...

2 Health and fitness

LISTENING Healthy alternatives? pp12–13

AIMS
The aims of this section are to help students practise critical thinking and
identify key vocabulary for listening. Additional aims are to help students
identify speakers' opinions, and learn and practise note-taking techniques.

LEAD IN
- Focus the students' attention on the page. Ask them to identify the skill
  LISTENING, and the topic (*Healthy alternatives*).
- Tell students to look at the photos. Ask them to think for a moment how the
  photos relate to the topic. Elicit ideas from some students.

PROCEDURE

1 🔘 **2.1** Students look at the photos again and read the instructions. Put them in
pairs to discuss the question. Students read the instructions for the listening
task. Play the CD. Check the answers as a class. **⚷ 1**

2 Put the students into small groups to discuss the questions. Encourage class
discussion, particularly of question 3 which brings in the concept of critical
thinking.

3 Students read the **STUDY SKILL** and the instructions, and do the task in pairs or
small groups. Elicit opinions from the class.

4 Students read the **STUDY SKILL** and the instructions, and match the words with
the definitions. Elicit answers from the students. **⚷ 4**

5 🔘 **2.2** Students read the **STUDY SKILL** and the instructions. Play the CD. Students
do the task. Get feedback from the whole class, encouraging the students to
remember any expressions which signalled or helped identify attitude. **⚷ 5**

6 🔘 **2.2** Tell the students they will listen to the same passage again. Students read
the instructions. Play the CD. Students identify which speaker mentions each
point. Check the answers together. **⚷ 6**

LISTENING Answer key pp12–13

⚷ 1
1 Acupuncture
2 Herbal medicine
3 Hydrotherapy
4 Hypnosis
5 Yoga

⚷ 4
1 h 2 c 3 b 4 d 5 g 6 e 7 a 8 f

⚷ 5
1 Sunil is undecided but thinks they should keep an open mind,
  Lee is in favour, and Miriam is against.
2 Lee.
3 Sunil and Miriam.

⚷ 6
1 S 2 L 3 L 4 M 5 S 6 L 7 M

Healthy body, healthy mind? pp14–15

1 Students read the instructions and answer the questions. ⚷1

2 💿 **2.3** Students read the instructions, listen to the CD, and do the task. ⚷2

3 💿 **2.4** Students read the instructions and listen to the CD. Check the answers as a class. ⚷3

4 Students read the **STUDY SKILL** and say what's wrong with the notes. Put the students in pairs to improve the notes. Get feedback from the whole class. ⚷4

5 💿 **2.5** Students read the instructions. Play the CD again. Students complete the notes. Elicit answers from the students. ⚷5

6 Students read the instructions and answer the questions in small groups. ⚷6

EXTENSION ACTIVITY

Write the topic, 'Physically fit students get better grades' on the board. Put students into pairs and ask them to think of 10 key words related to this topic. Students then listen to 💿 **2.5** and read the script on p59 to check how many of their key words were used and which other key words came up often (e.g. *performance, exercise, diet, success, research, weight, fitness, correlation, grade, score, etc.*).

RESEARCH References p15

AIMS
The aim of this section is to help students reference their information accurately.

LEAD IN
- Ask students to brainstorm possible research sources and write a list (*books, newspapers, journals, websites, etc.*).
- Put students in pairs or small groups to compare their lists.

PROCEDURE

1 Students read the **STUDY SKILL** and the instructions and do the task. Check the answers as a class. ⚷1

2 Students read the instructions and rewrite the information. Put the students in pairs to compare their answers, then elicit answers from some students. ⚷2

3 Put students in small groups. Students read the instructions and discuss the questions. Get feedback from the whole class.

4 Students read the instructions and use the resources available to carry out the task. Monitor and check the referencing carefully. Put the students in pairs or small groups to compare their sources and references.

EXTENSION ACTIVITY

Ask the students to rewrite their references from exercise 4 so that they are mixed up. Tell them to swap references with another student and see who can write them out in the correct order the fastest.

LISTENING Answer key pp14–15

⚷1

2 The research shows that fitter students do better.

⚷2

Students sit at their desks or computers for hours and live on very poor diets.

⚷3

1 F 2 T 3 F 4 T 5 T 6 F

⚷4

The notes are in full sentences and include unnecessary information.
Possible improvement
Study in Australia 2001 Dwyer & others
Correlation btwn academic performance + fitness
7,500 schoolchildren aged 7–15 tested
Questionnaires re. physical activity + fitness test results (running, jumping)
Academic performance measured 1–5 pts

⚷5

1 William McCarthy
2 California
3 Los Angeles
4 2002
5 2003
6 2,000
7 50
8 50
9 different
10 32
11 10
12 11
13 higher
14 lower
15 fitness
16 beneficial
17 academic

⚷6

1 There is a strong correlation between fitness and academic performance.
2 Students' own ideas.
3 Students' own answers.

RESEARCH Answer key p15

⚷1

1 Book: **author, year, title, publishing house**
2 Newspaper: **author, date of publication (year + month + day), title of article/headline, name of newspaper**
3 Journal: **author, year, title, journal name, journal number, chapter, page(s)**
4 Website: **author, year, title, date retrieved, website address**

⚷2

1 Journal: Campbell, T. & Hussain, A. (2011). Jurassic coast reveals more surprises. Geology Today, 14/2: 24–27
2 Book: Fantoni, L & Gale, S. (1997). Patterns in Pronunciation. Oxford, OUP
3 Newspaper: Odinga, J. (2010, January 23). Tourism set to increase over five years. Kenyan Daily News

SPEAKING Organizing a presentation p16

AIMS

The aims of this section are to help students organize a presentation and to help them focus on producing effective introductions.

LEAD IN

- Ask students to look at the photo and discuss with a partner where they think the woman is and what she is doing.
- Have a class discussion and encourage students briefly to share any experience they have of giving presentations.

PROCEDURE

1 Put the students into small groups. Ask them to read the instructions. Students discuss the questions and record their ideas. Elicit ideas and write them as spidergrams on the board.

2 Students read the instructions and discuss the quotation in the same groups as before.

3 🎧 **2.6** Students read the **STUDY SKILL** and the instructions. Play the CD. Students do the task. Elicit the answers from the class. ⌐ 3

4 Students read the instructions and do the matching task. Check the answers as a class. ⌐ 4

Introducing a presentation p17

1 Students read the instructions and discuss the questions in small groups. Get feedback from the whole class.

2 🎧 **2.7** Students read the **STUDY SKILL** and the instructions. Play the CD. Students do the task. Elicit answers from some students. ⌐ 2

3 Students read the instructions and look at the expressions in the Language Bank. Refer them back to the information they collected in the Research task. Students then do the task individually. Go round and monitor.

4 Students give their introductions to the class. Alternatively, they could do this in small groups.

5 Students read the instructions and give each other constructive feedback on their introductions.

ADDITIONAL PHOTOCOPIABLE ACTIVITY

Speaking 2 Introduction to a presentation

EXTENSION ACTIVITY

Students listen to 🎧 **2.6** again and read the audio script on p60. Ask them to underline words and expressions that signal which part of the presentation the excerpts are from (introduction, body or conclusion). They then check their findings together in small groups.

SPEAKING Answer key p16

⌐ 3

1 C   2 I   3 B   4 I   5 C

⌐ 4

A 3   B 4   C 5   D 1   E 2

SPEAKING Answer key p17

⌐ 2

- Introducing self (or others)
- Definitions
- Reasons
- Aim/Objective
- Plan

VOCABULARY DEVELOPMENT
Recording vocabulary p18

AIMS
The aim of this section is to help students record vocabulary effectively.

LEAD IN
- Put the students in small groups. Ask:
  – *Do you have a particular system for recording vocabulary?*
- Tell them to ask and answer this question within their groups.
- Have a class feedback session.

PROCEDURE
1 Students read the **STUDY SKILL**, the instructions, and discuss the questions in pairs. Check the answers together. ⌒ 1

2 Students read the instructions. In the same pairs, students discuss the questions and their ideas. Monitor carefully and elicit ideas from some students. ⌒ 2

3 Students read the instructions and do the task (on cards if they are available). In small groups, the students discuss their word cards and choose the ones which they think are well designed. Invite some students to show their chosen card and explain why they like the design.

4 Students read the **STUDY SKILL** and do the task individually or in pairs. Refer them to the scripts for 🔘 **2.1** and **2.2** on pp58–59 if they need help choosing vocabulary for the topic. You could display the vocabulary notebook pages around the walls for students to read. Alternatively, put them in small groups to show and explain their pages.

EXTENSION ACTIVITY
Ask the students to think about key words related to their own field of academic study and make a vocabulary notebook page or some word cards for their own words.

VOCABULARY DEVELOPMENT Answer key p18

⌒ 1

The words are organized alphabetically. A translation is given for each word.

⌒ 2

On one side: the word and its pronunciation are given.

On the other side: the part of speech, collocations, word family, definition, and example sentences are given.

Other possible information: translation.

REVIEW p19

AIMS

The aims of this section are to give students further practice in the skills learnt in this unit, and to give them the opportunity to review the work they have done. A further aim is to encourage students to apply what they have learnt to their other academic studies in English.

PROCEDURE

1 🔊 **2.8** Students read the instructions. Remind them that evaluating evidence is an important factor in critical thinking. Play the CD. Check the answers with the class. **○┐ 1**

2 🔊 **2.8** Students read the instructions. Check they know that they are going to listen to the same discussion again. Play the CD. Check the answers with the whole class, eliciting phrases that led them to the answers. **○┐ 2**

3 🔊 **2.9** Students read the instructions. Elicit 'dos and don'ts' for writing notes. Students complete the task. Check the answers as a class. **○┐ 3**

4 Students read the instructions and do the task. Check the references carefully with the class. **○┐ 4**

5 Students read the instructions and discuss the correct order in pairs. Elicit the answers. **○┐ 5**

6 In the same pairs, students read the instructions and do the task. Monitor carefully and if necessary, refer students back to the Language Bank on p17. Students read their introductions out to the class. Encourage constructive criticism.

EXTENSION ACTIVITY

Ask the students to list the skills they have learnt and practised in this unit. For example,
– critical thinking – evaluating evidence
– identifying speakers' opinions
– referencing research sources
– presentations – structure and introductions
– recording vocabulary

Put students in groups to discuss how to apply these skills to the work they do in their academic studies.

REVIEW   Answer key p19

○┐ 1

1 An article from a medical journal which explains that students should make sure they get enough protein.
2 A study which shows that students are eating more junk food than they did in the past.

○┐ 2

1 c   2 a   3 b

○┐ 3

First used: **by ancient Greeks, Romans, Chinese + others**
Reintroduced by: **Father Sebastian Kneipp, 19th century, Bavaria (Germany)**
Works by:
1 **using body's reaction to hot + cold – stimulates immune system/produces relaxing effects**
2 **toxins drawn out of body through baths, steam baths, saunas**
Treats: **back pain, anxiety, insomnia, arthritis**

○┐ 4

1 Kovak, M. (1994). Nutrition and the Brain. Vermont, USA, Allston College Press.
2 Reynolds, S. (2007). Sugar v Protein: How what we eat affects our performance. Retrieved November 25 2010 from: http://www.healthyacademia.co.uk/articles/sugarvprotein/

○┐ 5

1 'Hi. First a bit about myself – I'm Dr. Mark Sanchez from...'
2 'Today, I'm going to explain how conventional therapies and alternative therapies can be used together.'
3 'We realize that one of the biggest problems that we are facing is ...'
4 'The most obvious solution is to ...'
5 'So, to summarize, we need to be aware of ...'

3 Changing cities

LISTENING SKILLS Activating what you know • Critical thinking (3) Fact or opinion?
• Note-taking (2) linear notes • Recognizing signposts
SPEAKING SKILLS Expressing opinions • Presentations (3) Organizing the main content
VOCABULARY DEVELOPMENT Academic words

LISTENING The history of a city pp20–21

AIMS
The aims of this section are to help students activate what they already know to help them in listening, and to improve their critical thinking by differentiating between facts and opinions. Additional aims are to help students practise writing linear notes and recognize signposts in a lecture.

LEAD IN
• Put students in pairs. Ask:
  – *Which is better: living in a city or in the countryside?*
• Give them a minute to discuss the question and then elicit answers and reasons.

PROCEDURE

1 In pairs, students read the instructions and discuss the questions. Monitor and encourage discussion where necessary, then elicit answers from the class.

2 Students read the instructions and categorize the words in the box. They can use dictionaries if necessary. Put them in small groups to check their answers. You might also want to check the pronunciation of the vocabulary. **⚷ 2**

3 Students read the **STUDY SKILL**. You could highlight that preparing yourself before listening is an important stage. Students read the instructions and do the quiz. Encourage them to discuss how confident they feel about their answers, i.e. how much/little they know about the topic. Don't check the answers as a class at this stage.

4 Students read the instructions and do the task. Elicit answers from the class.
  ⚷ 4

5 **🔊 3.1** Students read the instructions. Play the CD. Students listen and check their answers to the quiz in exercise 3. **⚷ 5**

6 Students read the **STUDY SKILL** and the instructions and do the task. Elicit answers and ask them how they know which ones are opinions. **⚷ 6**

7 **🔊 3.1** Students read the instructions. Play the CD again. Students complete the notes. Put them in pairs to check the information in their notes. Monitor carefully. **⚷ 7**

8 Students read the instructions and discuss the questions in small groups. Get feedback from the whole class.

LISTENING Answer key pp20–21

⚷ 2

positive
sophisticated, bustling, cosmopolitan

negative
polluted, sprawling, congested, filthy, slums, overcrowded

neutral
urban, major, industrial, suburbs, capital

⚷ 4

1 He's a social historian.
2 It's about what happens to new migrants from rural areas when they move to megacities, like Mumbai and Lagos.
3 They provide sufficient infrastructure and social support to the poorest workers, who often build the growing cities.
4 It means the basic systems and structure that are necessary for a country or organization to run smoothly.

⚷ 5

1 c 2 a 3 d 4 b 5 d

⚷ 6

1 fact
2 opinion: I think Dubai is a successful city.
3 opinion: In my opinion, the centre of Moscow is too crowded.
4 opinion: I believe Mumbai will be an important cultural centre in the 21st century.
5 fact

⚷ 7

Causes of population growth
• **unemployed workers from rural areas moved to find work**
• **people coming from all over the newly developing British Empire**

Infrastructure improvements in 19th century London
• **the construction of roads and bridges**
• **the development of a public transport system**
• **the construction of a sewerage system**

Challenges of growth
• getting people from their homes to their job
• **poverty**
• **disease**

Eco-cities pp22–23

1 Put the students in pairs and ask them to look at the picture. Students read the instructions and discuss the questions. Elicit ideas from some students.

2 Students read the instructions and do the task. Ask them to compare their answers in pairs. **⊶ 2**

3 🔊 **3.2** Students read the **STUDY SKILL** and the instructions. Play the CD. The students correct the notes. Elicit the answers from the class. **⊶ 3**

4 🔊 **3.3** Students read the instructions. Play the CD. Students complete the notes.

5 Put students in pairs or small groups. They read the instructions and try to improve their notes. Go round and monitor. Get whole class feedback if necessary. You could invite students to come to the board and write up their notes. **⊶ 5**

6 🔊 **3.4** Students read the **STUDY SKILL** and the instructions. Tell them that they need to focus on the signposts used. Play the CD and students complete the task. **⊶ 6**

7 Students read the instructions. Put them in small groups to do the task. Ask one group to give their summary to the class.

EXTENSION ACTIVITY

Ask students to look again at the vocabulary in exercise 2 on p20. Put them in pairs and ask them to discuss which words they would use about Masdar City and why. Elicit ideas from the class.

LISTENING Answer key pp22–23

⊶ 2

Possible definitions

eco-city (n):	a city built on ecological principles which tries not to damage nature and the environment
minimization (n):	reduction to the lowest possible level
sustainable (adj):	using natural products/natural energy so it can go on for a long time without harming the environment
minimal (adj):	as little as possible, hardly any
renewable (adj):	able to be replaced naturally
emissions (n):	the sending out of harmful gases into the air
transition (n):	a change from one situation or state to another

⊶ 3

1 ecologically
2 as little impact as possible
3 produces no pollution at all
4 UAE
5 the UK
6 £10 & £20 billion

⊶ 5

Sources of energy:
1 **the sun – biggest solar farm in the Middle East**
2 **using mirrors to concentrate light, producing heat to drive generators**

Cooling of the city – by:
1 **design of the city with buildings close together providing plenty of shade**
2 **walls covered with terracotta mesh which keeps the sun out but lets wind through**
3 **wind towers which catch wind or breeze and direct it down into streets + buildings**

Transport in Masdar City:
walking everywhere
special 'podcars' – driverless vehicles powered by solar electricity
Future: **due to be finished 2020–2025. Clean air and minimal pollution**

⊶ 6

Definitions:	**Let's begin with** definitions…
Background:	**Let's turn to** Masdar City itself
Energy:	**Now what about** energy?
Cooling:	**Next, I'd like to look at** the cooling…
	1 **One method** is the design…
	2 **Secondly**, the walls…
	3 **A third solution proposed is** wind towers
Transport:	**What about** transport?
Future:	**So finally, what about** the future?

SPEAKING Expressing opinions p24

AIMS

The aim of this section is to help students express opinions and also organize the main content of their presentations.

LEAD IN

- Put students in pairs. Ask them to make a list of anything they know about Switzerland. Elicit ideas.

PROCEDURE

1 Students read the instructions and look at the photo. Put them in pairs to discuss the questions. Ask some students for feedback.

2 Students read the instructions and do the task individually. Put them in pairs to compare their choices and discuss their reasons. Get feedback from the class.

3 🔊 **3.5** Students read the **STUDY SKILL** and the instructions. Play the CD. Students answer the questions. Check the answers together. **🔑 3**

4 Put the students in small groups. Focus their attention on the Language Bank. Students read the instructions. Highlight that they should rank the factors and give reasons for their choices. Students do the task. Monitor the groups.

5 Students read the instructions and choose a member of their group to give a summary of their discussion.

Organizing content p25

1 Students look at the picture and read the instructions. Put them in pairs or small groups to do the task.

2 🔊 **3.6** Students read the instructions. Play the CD. Students do the task. Check the answers together. **🔑 2**

3 Put the students in small groups. Students read the instructions, choose a city and do the research task. Monitor and assist where necessary.

4 Students read the **STUDY SKILL** and the instructions. Tell them to think about the main content of their presentation and to divide it into different sections. Also remind them to use signposts. Students then prepare their presentation.

5 Focus students' attention on the Language Bank. Students read the instructions and take turns at giving their presentations.

6 Students read the instructions and the questions. Get feedback from the whole class on the presentations.

ADDITIONAL PHOTOCOPIABLE ACTIVITY

Speaking 3 Organizing a presentation

EXTENSION ACTIVITY

Students listen to 🔊 **3.5** again and read the audio script on p62. Ask them to underline all the phrases which introduce opinions. Then elicit answers.

Possible answers

I think it is / It seems to me that / ___ is not so important for me / as I see it / I really think / I don't think.

SPEAKING Answer key p24

🔑 3

1 Carlos.
2 Suzi.
3 Transport.
4 Suzi and Peter.
5 Carlos.

SPEAKING Answer key p25

🔑 2

1 Dubai.
2 Climate and public transport.
3 June, July and August are the hottest. February is the wettest.
4 First, I'd like to talk about
  Now let's turn to (the question of)

VOCABULARY DEVELOPMENT
Learning academic vocabulary p26

AIMS
The aims of this section are to help students improve their understanding and knowledge of academic vocabulary.

LEAD IN
- Focus the students' attention on the page and on the topic *(Learning academic vocabulary)*.
- Put students in pairs and ask them to think of ten words they would categorize as academic vocabulary and why.

PROCEDURE
1 Students read the **STUDY SKILL**. You could ask them to check whether any of the words they chose in the LEAD IN are technical words or general academic words.

Students read the instructions and do the matching task. Check answers as a class. **⌐1**

2 Students read the instructions and do the task. Invite students to read out their sentences. **⌐2**

3 Students read the instructions and do the task, using a dictionary when necessary. Check the answers together. **⌐3**

EXTENSION ACTIVITY
Students should find a short text from their own field of study and underline 5–10 academic words or phrases. Using a dictionary if necessary, they should prepare to give a brief summary of the main point of the article and explain the vocabulary to another student. Students can bring their texts into class and do the task in pairs.

VOCABULARY DEVELOPMENT Answer key p26

⌐1

1 e 2 g 3 b 4 a 5 f 6 d 7 c

⌐2

1 feasible
2 innovative
3 infrastructure
4 decline
5 context
6 receive
7 deteriorate

⌐3

1 discuss
2 divide
3 section
4 examine
5 assisted
6 pose
7 sufficient
8 define

REVIEW p27

AIMS

The aims of this section are to give students further practice in the skills learnt in this unit, and to give them the opportunity to review the work they have done. A further aim is to encourage students to apply what they have learnt to their other academic studies in English.

PROCEDURE

1 🔘 **3.7** Students read the instructions. You may need to explain that they need to write numbers in the boxes to show the order. Play the CD. Students do the task. Then they categorize the sentences with F (facts) or O (opinions). Elicit answers from the class. You could point out that the facts often have research or figures to back them up, whereas the opinions do not. 🔑 1

2 🔘 **3.8** Students read the instructions. Play the CD. Students complete the notes. Check the answers. 🔑 2

3 Students read the instructions and discuss the questions in pairs. Go round and monitor. You could ask them at the end whether their notes were good enough to help them in the discussion and what extra information they could have noted down.

4 Students read the instructions and do the task in pairs. Monitor carefully and refer them back to the Language Bank on p24 if necessary. You could put them in different pairs for further practice if there is time.

5 Students read the instructions and do the task. Check that they are using appropriate signposting language in their sentences. Elicit some of the best sentences as class feedback.

6 Students read the instructions and do the task individually. Check the answers as a class. 🔑 6

EXTENSION ACTIVITY

Ask the students to list the skills they have learnt and practised in this unit. For example,
– activating what they know (before listening)
– critical thinking – recognizing facts and opinions
– recognizing signposts in a presentation
– expressing opinions
– academic vocabulary

Put students in groups to discuss how to apply these skills to the work they do in their academic studies.

REVIEW Answer key p27

🔑 1

1	4	F
2	2	O
3	5	F
4	6	F
5	1	F
6	3	O

🔑 2

Topic: **Improvements being made to the city of London**

Transport problems: **small tunnels and old-fashioned trains, no air con, break down**

Improvements: **next 10 years – replace train carriages with spacious and more comfortable carriages, modernize stations**

Parks history: **belonged to monarch so building not allowed**

Improvements: **cycle paths, playgrounds + project to focus on places of historical significance inside parks and give visitor info**

🔑 6

1 obtained (received)
2 transformation (change)
3 strategies (plans)
4 data (information)
5 sector (part)

LISTENING SKILLS Recognizing causes and solutions • References to earlier comments • Listening to an illustrated talk
SPEAKING SKILLS Critical thinking (4) Seeing a problem from all sides • Pronunciation: numbers
• Presentations (4) Describing facts and figures
VOCABULARY DEVELOPMENT Collocations

LISTENING Feed the world pp28–29

AIMS
The aims of this section are to help students recognize signal words relating to causes and solutions and understand when a speaker is referring to an earlier comment. An additional aim is to help students listen to an illustrated talk.

LEAD IN
• Focus the students' attention on the page. Ask them to identify the skill LISTENING, and the topic (*Feed the world*).
• Split the class in half. One half should look at photo A, while the other half look at photo B. Give them 30 seconds to write a sentence describing their photo.
• Let them check their sentence with other students in their half of the class and choose which is the best. Elicit one sentence for each photo and write them on the board.

PROCEDURE
1 Students read the instructions and discuss the questions in pairs. Check answers with the whole class, asking a few different students about questions 3 and 4.

2 Students read the instructions and do the task. Check the answers. **O⊓ 2**

3 Students read the notes and check new vocabulary in a dictionary. Put them into groups to discuss the questions. Monitor and assist where necessary. Encourage class discussion to pool ideas.

4 🔊 **4.1** Students read the **STUDY SKILL** and read the instructions. Emphasize that they need to listen for the *causes* of the crisis. Play the CD. Students listen and take notes. **O⊓ 4**

5 🔊 **4.2** Students read the instructions. Check that they know they are listening for the *solutions* to the crisis. Play the CD. **O⊓ 5**

6 Students read the instructions and discuss the questions in pairs. Monitor and check that they have taken sufficient notes from exercises 4 and 5 to do the task.

7 Students read the **STUDY SKILL** and the instructions and do the task. Ask them to check their underlining with a partner. Elicit and write the references on the board. **O⊓ 7**

8 🔊 **4.2** Students read the instructions. Play the CD again. Students do the task. Check the answers as a class. **O⊓ 8**

9 Put the students into groups of three or four. Ask them to read the instructions and evaluate each of the three possible solutions in turn. Discuss their evaluations as a whole class.

LISTENING Answer key pp28–29

O⊓ 2
1 B   2 A   3 A   4 B   5 B   6 B   7 B   8 A   9 A   10 A

O⊓ 4

Possible answers
– Low productivity of farmers: can't afford seeds/fertilizer/water for irrigation
– Natural causes: climate change = drought in Australia and Europe
– Population growth: greater demand
– Production of biofuels: crops for fuel instead of food

O⊓ 5

Possible answers
– Make world's crops 'weather-proof', e.g. in Africa make a farm pond to collect water in wet season.
– Stop investment in biofuels.
– Increase productivity by giving farmers seeds/fertilizer/water.

O⊓ 7
1 As I said earlier,
2 I'd just like to reiterate that
3 I'd just like to come back to what (Tom) said about
4 I think (Laura) made a good point about

O⊓ 8
1 c   2 d   3 b   4 a

Malawi – a success story pp30–31

1 Students read the instructions. Put them into small groups to brainstorm their ideas about Malawi using the prompts in the box.

2 🔊 **4.3** Students read the instructions. Ask them to decide if they are listening for gist or specific information (*gist*). Play the CD and the students do the task. Check the answer. 🔑 **2**

3 🔊 **4.4** Students read the **STUDY SKILL** and read the instructions. Play the CD. Students complete the handout and check their answers in pairs. Monitor and elicit class feedback. 🔑 **3**

4 🔊 **4.5** Students read the instructions. Play the CD. They do the task. Check answers together. 🔑 **4**

5 🔊 **4.6** Students read the instructions. Play the CD and students complete the graph. Show the completed graph on the board if possible or elicit the information. 🔑 **5**

6 Students read the instructions and discuss the questions in small groups. Go round and monitor, encouraging discussion where necessary.

EXTENSION ACTIVITY

Students read the audio script for 🔊 **4.5** and **4.6** on p63. Ask them to underline all the phrases where the speaker draws attention to the slides and any phrases where he refers to a comment made earlier. Check together.

Answers

Here you can see/This slide shows/As you can see from the graph/As I said at the beginning.

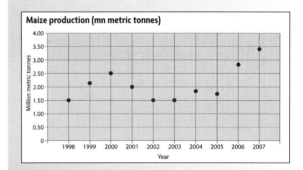

SPEAKING Discussing pros and cons p32

AIMS

The aim of this section is to encourage students to see a problem from all sides and also present facts and figures clearly. A further aim is to improve students' pronunciation of numbers.

LEAD IN

- Ask the students to brainstorm what they understand about the term 'biofuel'.
- Elicit ideas and write them on the board.

PROCEDURE

1 🔊 **4.7** Students read the instructions and the questions. Play the CD. Students listen and answer the questions. Encourage them to check their answers with a partner. Then get feedback from the whole class. (An OHT of the flow-chart would be useful.) 🗝 **1**

2 Students read the **STUDY SKILL** and the instructions. Put them in pairs to discuss the advantages and disadvantages of biofuels. Elicit some ideas from the class. 🗝 **2**

3 🔊 **4.8** Students read the instructions. Play the CD. Students listen and do the task. Check the answers. 🗝 **3**

4 Put the students in small groups of three or four. Ask them to read the instructions and prepare to do the task. Focus their attention on the Language Bank. Students then discuss the topic. Go round and monitor.

5 Students read the instructions and appoint one person. Ask them to present their summaries to the class.

Presenting facts and figures p33

1 🔊 **4.9** Students read the **STUDY SKILL** and the instructions. Play the CD. Students do the task and practise saying the numbers in pairs. Write the answers on the board for clarity. Go round and monitor when they are saying the numbers out loud. Check that the stress and pauses are in the right places. 🗝 **1**

2 🔊 **4.10** Students read the instructions and look at the headings. Play the CD and students do the task. Elicit the answers and write them on the board. 🗝 **2**

ADDITIONAL PHOTOCOPIABLE ACTIVITY

Speaking 4 Summarizing

3 Students work in groups of three. Ask them to read the **STUDY SKILL** and the instructions. In their groups they should choose three different countries. Students prepare a talk on their country using the table and the Language Bank expressions. Give them a time limit. Go round and monitor carefully.

4 Students take it in turns to give their talks. The other students in their group should practise taking notes. Give constructive criticism on the presentations at the end.

EXTENSION ACTIVITY

Put the students in pairs. Ask them to think of a topic where there are arguments for and against and write it on a slip of paper. Swap the slips of paper with another pair. Students discuss the pros and cons of the issue in their pairs, using the expressions from the Language Bank on p32. Monitor and give feedback.

Possible topics

going on a gap year/the Internet/identity cards/animal testing/nuclear power/GM food/home schooling

---

SPEAKING Answer key p32

🗝 **1**

1 Fuel from crops.
2 Ethanol from sugar cane and grains, and biodiesel from oil palm and soybean.
3 Brazil, the USA, and France.
4 Transport – cars/lorries/buses/planes.
5 crops harvested → transported to bio-refinery → converted to ethanol → fuel distributed → biofuel sold

🗝 **2**

Possible answers

Advantages: renewable, cheap, bring money to the economy of the country where they are grown, can be used in that country so no shipping costs (unlike oil)

Disadvantages: take up space where food crops could be grown, food crops become more expensive as scarce

🗝 **3**

1 Hiroto.
2 Mike.
3 Samira.

SPEAKING Answer key p33

🗝 **1**

1 109,773
2 15,675,020
3 36%
4 78.95
5 0.245
6 ¾

🗝 **2**

Country: <u>Tunisia</u>
Location: <u>North Africa, between Algeria (West) and Libya (East)</u>
Area sq km: <u>163,610</u>
Population: <u>10,175,014 in 2006</u>
Climate: <u>mild winter, lots of rain, hot dry summer in the north / hot and dry all year in the south</u>
Life expectancy: <u>75.12 years</u>
Main crops: <u>wheat: 1,360,000 metric tonnes</u>
<u>tomatoes: 920,000 metric tonnes</u>
<u>olives: 700,000 metric tonnes</u>

VOCABULARY DEVELOPMENT Collocations p34

AIMS
The aim of this section is to improve students' knowledge and understanding of collocations.

LEAD IN
- Write 'collocation' and 'to collocate with' on the board.
- Elicit the parts of speech (*noun, and verb + preposition*) and ask whether anyone can give a definition. If not, give the explanation yourself.

PROCEDURE

1 Students read the **STUDY SKILL** and the instructions, and complete the table. Ask them to share their ideas with a partner. Draw the table on the board and invite students to come up and write in the spaces. 🔑 1

2 Students read the instructions and complete the task. There is a wide range of possible sentences so monitor this carefully. Elicit some sentences as feedback. 🔑 2

3 Students read the instructions and do the task. Elicit answers from the class. 🔑 3

EXTENSION ACTIVITY
Students read audio script 4.1 on p62. Remind them that the topic is the Global Food Crisis. Ask them to make a list of 5–10 key collocations from this audio script which they could learn in order to speak about this topic in the future.

Possible answers

low productivity/natural causes/climate change/global production/population growth/food prices/produce crops

cause a crisis/find a solution/contribute to a problem/have a huge impact on/ consider a solution

VOCABULARY DEVELOPMENT Answer key p34

🔑 1

Possible answers
a problem: face, contribute to, solve, tackle
a solution: find, consider, look into
a conclusion: reach, draw, come to
a discussion: have, summarize, start
crops: grow, harvest, produce, irrigate

🔑 2

Possible answers
1 Malawi is solving the problem of a lack of water.
2 Scientists are considering a solution to (the effects of) global warming.
3 The meeting drew to a conclusion.
4 The staff is having a discussion about salaries.
5 Malawi grows crops such as maize and tea.

🔑 3

1 grave/major/serious/severe/terrible
2 caused/created/led to/precipitated/provoked/sparked off
3 during
4 point
5 confidence

REVIEW p35

AIMS

The aims of this section are to give students further practice in the skills learnt in this unit, and to give them the opportunity to review the work they have done. A further aim is to encourage students to apply what they have learnt to their other academic studies in English.

PROCEDURE

1 🔘 **4.11** Students read the instructions. Play the CD. They listen and do the task. Elicit the answers. ⊙─ **1**

2 🔘 **4.11** Students read the instructions. Tell them that they are going to hear the same presentation again. Play the CD. They listen and do the task. Check the answers. ⊙─ **2**

3 Students read the instructions and complete the table individually. ⊙─ **3**

4 Students discuss the topics from exercise 3 in pairs. You could also refer them back to the Language Bank on p32. Give students a time limit to discuss each topic. Go round and monitor. At the end, elicit feedback from some pairs. Also, ask how well they feel they used the expressions for discussing pros and cons.

EXTENSION ACTIVITY

Ask the students to list the skills they have learnt and practised in this unit. For example,
– recognizing causes and solutions
– listening to an illustrated talk
– discussing pros and cons
– describing facts and figures in a presentation
– developing understanding and knowledge of collocations

Put students in groups to discuss how to apply these skills to the work they do in their academic studies.

REVIEW Answer key p35

⊙─ **1**

1 1.1 billion people worldwide don't have sufficient access to safe, clean drinking water.
2 Deforestation (because trees hold water in the ground and removing them reduces the amount of underground water).
3 Educating citizens and governments about the serious effects of deforestation.

⊙─ **2**

Slides 2 and 3.

⊙─ **3**

Students' own ideas.

5 Global culture

LISTENING SKILLS Listening for questions • Critical thinking (5) Anecdotal evidence
• Recognizing what information is important
SPEAKING SKILLS Conducting interviews • Presenting with graphics
VOCABULARY DEVELOPMENT Suffixes

LISTENING Are we all becoming the same? pp36–37

AIMS

The aims of this section are to help students practise listening for questions and also to recognize anecdotal evidence.

LEAD IN

- Focus the students' attention on the page. Ask them to identify the skill **LISTENING**, and the topic (*Are we all becoming the same?*).
- Put students in pairs. Ask them to find out two things they have in common with their partner. Elicit whether they think they are similar to their partner or very different.

PROCEDURE

1 Put the students into small groups. Ask them to read the instructions and discuss the question. Ask some students for their definitions.

2 Students read the instructions and do the quiz individually. They then use the key to calculate their personal score. Get some quick feedback from the whole class, including cultural references if necessary.

Cultural references
 – *House* is an American television medical drama.
 – Bollywood films are Hindi-language films, which include singing and dancing.
 – Starbucks is the largest coffeehouse company in the world.
 – Lionel Messi, born 20 June 1987 in Argentina, is considered one of the best football players of his generation.
 – Facebook is a social networking site.
 – Jimmy Choo is a famous shoe designer.

3 Put the students back into their small groups. They read the instructions and discuss the questions. Go round and monitor. Get feedback from the class.

4 Students read the instructions and the text. Put them in pairs to discuss the questions. Get feedback from the class. **⊙ 4**

5 **5.1** Students read the **STUDY SKILL** and the instructions. Play the CD. Students do the task. Check the answers. **⊙ 5**

6 **5.1** Students read the instructions. Explain that they are going to hear the same discussion again. Play the CD. Students do the task. Elicit the answers from some students. **⊙ 6**

7 **5.2** Students read the instructions. Say that they are going to hear part of the same discussion again. Play the CD. Students decide if the speakers are in favour, against or neutral. Check the answers. **⊙ 7**

8 **5.3** Students read the **STUDY SKILL**. Check the pronunciation and meaning of 'anecdotal', if necessary. Students read the instructions. Play the CD. Students do the task.

9 Students check their answers in pairs, then read the instructions and discuss the questions. Get feedback from the whole class to find out their ideas. **⊙ 9**

LISTENING Answer key pp36–37

⊙ 4
Possible answers
1 – 'cultural boundaries': differences between cultures
   – 'Western ideals': consumerism, human rights, equality, democracy, capitalism, emphasis on the individual, freedom of speech
   – 'sense of community': a positive feeling of belonging to a group of people
2 Global culture will either destroy local cultures, languages and communities, or it will have positive effects such as shared values and political unity.

⊙ 5
1 how do you see it?
2 What do the rest of you think?
3 what's your view on this?
4 Would anyone like to comment?
5 what's your view on this?

⊙ 6
NB some views are held by more than one speaker
1 Jane: c, f,
2 Lee: a, b, g
3 Miriam: d, f
4 Sunil: e, g

⊙ 7
Jane: neutral
Lee: in favour
Miriam: against
Sunil: in favour

⊙ 9
fashion-designer labels: factual
the TV programme *House*: factual
Pizza Hut: factual
Russian food: anecdotal
the film – *Avatar*: anecdotal

Possible answers
– Anecdotal evidence can be backed up with factual or scientific evidence.
– Factual evidence could include research results, figures, dates. Scientific evidence could include results of tests and experiments.

Coffee and culture pp38–39

1 Students read the instructions and discuss the questions in groups. Get feedback from the class. 🔑 1

2 Students read the instructions and choose topics for the talk. Elicit answers from the students. 🔑 2

3 Students read the instructions and do the task. Find out which students chose the same lecture title and group them together to compare their questions.

4 Students read the instructions and predict the lecturer's questions. Ask them to compare their ideas in pairs. You could elicit some questions and write them on the board. 🔑 4

5 🎵 **5.4** Students read the instructions. Play the CD. Elicit answers for the questions on the board. Ask whether any other questions were answered. 🔑 5

6 🎵 **5.5** Students read the **STUDY SKILL**. You could ask the students if they have noticed or used any of these clues in talks they've heard or given.

Students read the instructions. Point out that they are only going to hear the introduction of the talk. Play the CD. Get feedback from the whole class. 🔑 6

7 🎵 **5.6** Students read the instructions. Play the CD. Students listen and complete the notes. Ask them to compare answers in pairs before eliciting answers from some students. 🔑 7

8 🎵 **5.7** Students read the instructions. Play the CD. Students write notes.

9 Students read the instructions and answer the questions. Put them in pairs to check their answers. Monitor carefully and check the answers as a class. 🔑 9

10 Students read the instructions and do the discussion task in small groups of three or four. Have a class discussion.

EXTENSION ACTIVITY

Students listen again to the whole talk 🎵 **5.4** and read the audio script on p65. Ask them to underline ways in which the speaker highlights important information. Refer them to the Study Skill on p38 if necessary.

Possible answers

repetition and spelling of key name 'Schultz'

repetition of figures: '1,200 new stores every year – that's 1,200' and '30,000'

signal expressions: 'What does it all mean?' and 'That last point is quite important.'

LISTENING Answer key pp38–39

🔑 1

Possible answers

1 People like coffee/a meeting place outside your home/relaxing and informal.

2 For: you feel comfortable travelling anywhere because there's a place you know and you know what you're going to get. Against: local meeting places may not be able to do business/We are all becoming the same.

🔑 2

Possible answers

Global marketing, Advantages of going global, International brands, The growth of global companies.

🔑 4

Possible questions

1 How many coffee shops does Starbucks have?
2 When did the first Starbucks coffee shop open?
3 Who started Starbucks?
4 How many countries is Starbucks in?
5 What makes Starbucks so popular?

🔑 5

Possible answers

1 Over 16,000.
2 1986.
3 Howard Schultz.
4 50.
5 It sees itself as 'a familiar place in a new city'.

🔑 6

Possible answers

1 The speaker pauses before the phrase, speaks more slowly and clearly, and says he has used the phrase before in a previous lecture.
2 The speaker speaks slowly and clearly, and the word 'Starbucks' is mentioned twice.
3 The speaker speaks slowly and clearly.

🔑 7

1 Seattle	6 1996	11 6,400
2 1982	7 Tokyo, Japan	12 2001
3 Schultz	8 1998	13 2004
4 1987	9 UK	14 1,200
5 North America	10 2003	

🔑 9

1 There are over 16,000 stores in 50 countries.
2 There are plans for 30,000 stores worldwide.
3 China.
4 Stores are a welcoming place to meet friends/family, read books, and are a familiar place in a new city.
5 Some people think that they're bad for local businesses because they cannot compete, and the choice is also limited as all coffee shops will be the same.
6 Supporters say they're giving people what they want, i.e. comfortable coffee shops to meet friends, enjoy coffee, and use their laptops.
7 All over the world people can get the same product and the same standard of service.

SPEAKING Conducting an interview p40

AIMS
The aims of this section are to help students conduct interviews and also practise using graphics when giving presentations.

LEAD IN
- Focus the students' attention on the page. Ask them to look at the photo and discuss with a partner where it was taken and what it shows.

PROCEDURE
1 Students read the instructions and discuss the questions in pairs. Get feedback from the whole class.

2 Students read the instructions and match the questions with the question types. Check the answers. **⊶ 2**

3 Students read the instructions and do the task in pairs. Check the answers as a class. **⊶ 3**

4 🎧 **5.8** Students read the **STUDY SKILL** and the instructions. Play the CD. Students do the task. Elicit answers from the class. **⊶ 4**

5 Students read the instructions and do the task individually. Give them a time limit. Monitor carefully and assist where necessary.

6 Students read the instructions and do the task in pairs. Go round and monitor. Get feedback from the class and elicit which questions worked well and which needed to be changed.

7 Students read the instructions. Ask them to move around the classroom and interview five or six different students. Tell them that they will need the results for a presentation. Monitor carefully.

Presenting results p41
1 Students read the instructions, and discuss and order the factors in pairs. Get feedback from the class.

2 Students read the **STUDY SKILL** and read the instructions. Set a reasonable time limit. Students work individually to do the task. Monitor and assist where necessary.

3 🎧 **5.9** Students read the instructions and look at the graphics. Play the CD. Students label the graphics. Check the answers together. (It would be helpful to have the completed graphics prepared on an OHT.) **⊶ 3**

4 Students read the instructions. Focus their attention on the Language Bank. Students give their presentations to the class. Tell the class to take notes and ask questions. Give constructive feedback on the presentations.

EXTENSION ACTIVITY
Students listen to 🎧 **5.9** again and read the audio script on p66. Ask them to circle adverbs which the speaker uses to highlight specific information.

Answers
surprisingly, interestingly, clearly, noticeably

SPEAKING Answer key p40

⊶ 2
1 open questions
2 Yes/No
3 multiple choice
4 rating questions

⊶ 3
1 Yes/No, multiple choice, rating questions
2 open questions
3 multiple choice, rating questions
4 multiple choice, yes/no, rating questions

⊶ 4
1 Yes.
2 No ('Why do you like shopping here?').
3 Yes ('Do you live in Manchester?').
4 No – not necessary.

SPEAKING Answer key p41

⊶ 3
1
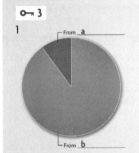

2
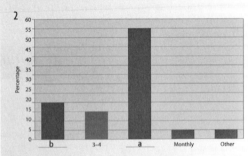

3
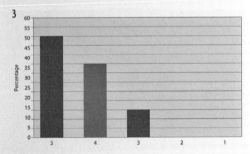

4 1 walking
   2 car
   3 bus
   4 other

VOCABULARY DEVELOPMENT Word formation (1) p42

AIMS

The aim of this section is to improve students' understanding of how words are formed using suffixes.

LEAD IN

• Write the word 'suffix' on the board and ask whether anybody knows what it means or can give any examples of suffixes. Write any good suggestions on the board.

PROCEDURE

1 Students read the **STUDY SKILL** and the instructions, and do the task, using a dictionary. Check the answers together. It would be useful to highlight the word stress. **⊙┑ 1**

2 Students read the instructions and do the task. Ask them to check with a partner. Monitor carefully, especially for pronunciation and spelling. Check the answers as a class. **⊙┑ 2**

3 Students read the instructions and do the task. Point out that there may be more or fewer than three words in each column. Elicit answers and write them on the board to ensure correct spelling. **⊙┑ 3**

4 Students read the instructions and do the discussion task in small groups.

EXTENSION ACTIVITY

Ask the students to think about key words related to their own field of academic study and write down the other words in each word family which can be formed using suffixes.

VOCABULARY DEVELOPMENT Answer key p42

⊙┑ 1

1 Westernize, Westernization
2 internationalize, internationalization
3 standardize, standardization
4 liberalize, liberalization
5 modernize, modernization
6 industrialize, industrialization
7 formalize, formalization

⊙┑ 2

neurology:	**noun**	**neurologist**	**noun**
plagiarize:	**verb**	**plagiarism**	**noun**
serious:	**adjective**	**seriousness**	**noun**
power:	**noun**	**powerless**	**adjective**
treat	**verb/noun**	**treatment**	**noun**

⊙┑ 3

-able:	**enjoyable, changeable, sociable**
-ist:	**tourist, socialist, mannerist**
-ism:	**heroism, tourism, socialism, mannerism**
-ness:	**calmness, hardness, happiness, cleanliness**
-less:	**aimless, helpless, changeless**
-ment:	**containment, arrangement, enjoyment, improvement, equipment**

REVIEW p43

AIMS

The aims of this section are to give students further practice in the skills learnt in this unit, and to give them the opportunity to review the work they have done. A further aim is to encourage students to apply what they have learnt to their other academic studies in English.

PROCEDURE

1 5.10 Students read the instructions. Play the CD. Check the answers with the class. 🔑 1

2 5.11 Students read the instructions. Play the CD. Elicit the answers from some students. Also, ask them how the speaker highlighted the important information (*repetition, slowing down, emphasis*). 🔑 2

3 Students read the instructions and do the task. Ask them to check their answers with a partner and then elicit answers as a class. 🔑 3

4 Students read the instructions and work in pairs to interview each other. Monitor carefully.

5 In the same pairs, students read the instructions and discuss how they would explain the graphs in a presentation. Ask one or two students to demonstrate.

6 Students read the instructions and do the exercise. Check answers as a class. 🔑 6

ADDITIONAL PHOTOCOPIABLE ACTIVITY

Speaking 5 Talking about charts

EXTENSION ACTIVITY

Ask the students to list the skills they have learnt and practised in this unit. For example,
– critical thinking – anecdotal evidence
– recognizing what information is important
– conducting interviews to get data
– using graphics in presentations
– understanding and using suffixes

Put students in groups to discuss how to apply these skills to the work they do in their academic studies.

REVIEW Answer key p43

🔑 1

1 C   2 A   3 B

🔑 2

Founded: **1943 by Ingvar Kamprad**
First store (in Sweden): **Almhult, 1958**
First international store: **Norway, 1963**
Currently: **250 stores in over 40 countries**

🔑 3

Students' own questions.

🔑 6

1 (standard)**ize**
2 (help)**less**
3 (special)**ist**
4 (Encourage)**ment**
5 (hard)**ness**

6 History and heritage

LISTENING What is 'World Heritage'? pp44–45

AIMS
The aims of this section are to help students establish criteria and detect speakers' points of view and assumptions.

LEAD IN
- Focus the students' attention on the page. Ask them to identify the skill **LISTENING**, and the topic (*What is 'World Heritage'?'*).
- Put them in pairs. Ask them to give a brief description of the biggest tourist attraction in their country, and why people want to visit it. Also ask them which is the oldest place in their country and whether tourists often go there. Elicit some ideas.

PROCEDURE
1 In pairs, students read the instructions and discuss the definition of 'heritage' and their understanding of 'World Heritage'. Clarify as a class what it means.
🔑 1

2 Students read the instructions and match the photos with the names. Check answers as a class 🔑 2

3 Students read the **STUDY SKILL** and the instructions, and discuss the sites in small groups. Monitor and encourage where necessary. Get feedback from the class and write possible criteria on the board. They will research the UNESCO criteria in more detail later in the unit.

4 Students read the instructions. They first do the task individually, then check with a partner and discuss which buildings meet the criteria. Elicit some ideas.

5 Students read the instructions and the notes and answer the questions. Check the answers together. 🔑 5

6 Students read the instructions and do the task. Ask them to compare their questions in pairs. Elicit questions to write on the board. 🔑 6

7 💿 **6.1** Students read the instructions. Play the CD. Students do the task then check with a partner. 🔑 7

8 💿 **6.2** Students read the instructions. Explain that they are going to hear part of the same discussion again. Play the CD. Students listen and correct the fact sheet. Check the answers. 🔑 8

9 💿 **6.3** Students read the instructions. Play the CD. Students do the task and check their answers with a partner. Monitor carefully and check answers as a class. 🔑 9

LISTENING Answer key pp44–45

🔑 **1**
(Simplified from the UNESCO website) 'World Heritage' = Any man-made or natural place or feature which is of outstanding universal value from the point of view of history, art, science or conservation.

🔑 **2**
1 B   2 C   3 D   4 A

🔑 **5**
1 Dr Tomas Olearski.
2 UNESCO.
3 How UNESCO decides which sites should be protected and what it means to be selected as a World Heritage site.

🔑 **6**
Possible questions
– When and where did the World Heritage programme start?
– Who started it?
– How many World Heritage sites are there now?
– Are all the countries in the world part of the programme?
– Why do you think the World Heritage programme is important?
– How are World Heritage sites chosen?

🔑 **7**
1 Mainly factual/information.
2 Students' own answers.

🔑 **8**
Initial idea came in <u>1954</u> (not 1972)
Initial project: to move the <u>**Abu Simbel and Philae Temple complexes**</u> (not the Pyramids) because of the <u>**Aswan High Dam project**</u> (not the rising level of the Nile)
More than <u>**$80 million**</u> (not $8million) collected from UN members
The convention was ratified in <u>1972</u> (not 1987)
Goal: to <u>**preserve**</u> (not build) heritage sites...
Convention ratified by <u>187</u> (not 87) countries

🔑 **9**
1   911
2   704
3   180
4   27
5   151
6   Sydney Opera House/Abu Simbel Temples/Verona/Hiroshima Peace Memorial
7   Tropical rainforest of Sumatra/Mount Kenya/Lake Baikal
8   Cappadocia in Turkey
9   10
10 tentative
11 nomination
12 the World Heritage Committee

Conserving a historical site pp46–47

1 Students read the instructions and questions. Check the words 'renovation' and 'drawbacks' if necessary. Students do the discussion task in small groups. Elicit some ideas from the students. 🔑1

2 🎧 **6.4** Students read the instructions. Play the CD. Elicit words from the students and write them on the board.

3 🎧 **6.5** Students read the instructions. Play the CD. Students do the task. Check the answers together. 🔑3

4 🎧 **6.5** Students read the instructions and the statements. Play the CD. Students do the task.

5 Students check answers in pairs. Monitor carefully. Check the answers as a class. 🔑5

6 🎧 **6.5** Students read the **STUDY SKILL** and the instructions and do the task. 🔑6

7 Students read the instructions and discuss their answers in small groups. They give their opinions with examples. Get feedback from the class.

8 Students read the instructions and do the task in pairs. Elicit answers from some students. 🔑8

ADDITIONAL PHOTOCOPIABLE ACTIVITY

Speaking 6 Finding hidden assumptions

EXTENSION ACTIVITY

Put students in pairs. Ask them to write some more titles for talks or presentations based on particular assumptions (perhaps related to their own field of study). Then instruct them to swap their titles with another pair and see if they can identify the assumptions.

RESEARCH Using the Internet p47

AIMS

The aim of this section is to help students use websites from organizations or companies for research purposes.

LEAD IN

• Ask students to brainstorm what they think the UNESCO website address is.

PROCEDURE

1 Students read the **STUDY SKILL** and the instructions and do the task. (If computer access is restricted within the class, the teacher should access the website beforehand and print off the relevant pages.) Check the answers as a class. 🔑1

2 Put the students in groups of four. They read the instructions and each group member chooses a different site. Using the UNESCO website, students do the task individually then use their notes to describe their site to the group. Monitor carefully.

3 Students read the instructions and do the task individually either in the lesson or as homework. Ask students to produce presentations or pieces of written work to bring to class.

EXTENSION ACTIVITY

Students produce a brief list of the most important organization or company websites relating to their field of study. Ask them to look at the websites and assess them in terms of ease or difficulty of use for research purposes.

LISTENING Answer key pp46–47

🔑1

Possible answers
1 brick, mud, stone
2 It was falling down/deteriorating and it is an important site – historical interest.
3 Possible drawbacks: Very expensive. May not look authentic – can't find original materials or don't know or can't use the original methods for repairing it. Some deterioration over the years is natural so it's strange if it looks new.

🔑3

3 Bahla market
2 The oasis from the top of Bahla
5 The fort under renovation
1 Bahla – the oasis town
4 Bahla Fort viewed from the market

🔑5

1 F: The main agricultural crop is dates.
2 T
3 T
4 F: It is the oldest and the largest.
5 F: In 13th or 14th century so it's about 700 years ago.
6 T
7 F: $9 million was spent by the Omani Govt, not UNESCO.
8 F: It was removed from the endangered buildings list in 2004.
9 F: Mud and stone.
10 T

🔑6

1 Restoration has been a long and expensive procedure, and will attract tourism.
2 Possible assumptions are:
 – the Bahla fort deserves to be a World Heritage site.
 – the site would have been lost without UNESCO
 – restoration, being a World Heritage site, and being a tourist attraction are all good.

🔑8

Possible answers
1 Forming a study group is a good idea.
2 You should avoid plagiarism.
3 Students should try to keep fit.
4 The Internet should be introduced into schools.
5 Developing countries need to be sent aid.

RESEARCH Answer key p47

🔑1

1 10.
2 6 cultural and 4 natural.
3 Yes.
4 Cultural: to be an outstanding example of a type of building, architectural or technological ensemble or landscape which illustrates (a) significant stage(s) in human history.
 Natural: to contain superlative natural phenomena or areas of exceptional natural beauty and aesthetic importance.

SPEAKING Presenting data p48

AIMS
The aims of this section are to help students present data and practise concluding their presentations.

LEAD IN
- Put the students in pairs and ask them to brainstorm the ways in which data can be presented graphically (*chart, graph, pie chart, etc.*).

PROCEDURE
1 Students read the instructions and do the task individually before comparing ideas in pairs. Elicit the answers and get feedback from the class. **o─ 1**

2 **6.6** Students read the **STUDY SKILL** and the instructions. Play the CD. Students do the task. Elicit feedback as a class. **o─ 2**

3 **6.6** Students read the instructions. Play the CD again. Students do the task and then discuss their answers with a partner. Monitor carefully and elicit answers as a class. **o─ 3**

4 Put the students in groups of three. They read the instructions and each student in the group chooses a different table. Give them a time limit, then monitor and assist as they prepare their talks. Students give their talks to their group. Encourage constructive criticism of how they presented their data.

Concluding your presentation p49

1 Students read the instructions and discuss the questions in small groups. (The answers are in the Study Skill – see exercise 2).

2 Students read the **STUDY SKILL** and the instructions. In their groups, they do the discussion task. Get feedback from the class and write ideas on the board.

3 **6.7** Students read the instructions. Play the CD. Students do the task. Elicit ideas from some students. **o─ 3**

4 Students read the instructions. Focus their attention on the Language Bank. Give the students a time limit and monitor their preparation carefully.

5 Students give their presentations to the class. Tell the class to take notes and ask questions. Give constructive feedback on the presentations.

EXTENSION ACTIVITY
Ask the students to collect data related to an aspect of their own specific studies. Tell them they should prepare a table similar to the ones on p48 and plan how they would present the data in a talk. Give feedback on their plans or, if time permits, they could give their presentations to the class.

SPEAKING Answer key p48

o─ 1

It shows the number of World Heritage sites in different continents and categorizes them as natural, cultural or mixed sites.
Main points: Students should point out highs and lows from the table.

o─ 2

Talk B is better because the speaker gives a more considered analysis of the table. Speaker A simply goes through the table line by line describing all the data.

o─ 3

Speaker A does not give the title of the table or explain what it is about. He just reads from left to right across the table. He does not select any specific data or make any comparisons.

Speaker B gives the title of the table and explains the purpose. She picks out highs and lows in the data, highlighting interesting figures and drawing conclusions about them. She goes from general (totals) to specific (regions, highs and lows).

SPEAKING Answer key p49

o─ 3

Talk C is the best conclusion. 'To sum up' is a clear signal that this is the concluding part. The speaker summarizes the main points, using clear sequencing phrases to refer back to the talk. The ending is strong and reiterates the purpose of the talk. The speaker also invites questions.

Talk A does not summarize and introduces new information.

Talk B is better but does not mention the purpose of the talk and the ending is not strong.

VOCABULARY DEVELOPMENT Word formation (2) p50

AIMS
The aim of this section is to improve students' understanding of how words are formed using prefixes.

LEAD IN
- Write the word 'prefix' on the board and ask whether anybody knows what it means or can give any examples of prefixes.
- Write any good suggestions on the board.

PROCEDURE
1 Students read the **STUDY SKILL** and the instructions and do the task. Check the answers together. ⊶ 1

2 Students read the instructions and do the task, using a dictionary if necessary. Check the answers as a class and elicit the meanings of the prefixes in the words given. ⊶ 2

EXTENSION ACTIVITY
Ask the students to brainstorm other words which are formed using the prefixes in exercises 1 and 2. Give them a time limit then put them into pairs or small groups to compare ideas. If time permits, ask some of them to come to the board and write their words up.

VOCABULARY DEVELOPMENT Answer key p50

⊶ 1
1 not meet the requirements
2 see before
3 cannot be maintained
4 think again about something
5 form an opinion before seeing the evidence
6 below the earth
7 give out in a different way
8 not easy to believe

⊶ 2
1 extracurricular (*extra-* : outside/beyond)
2 overestimated (*over-* : too much/more than usual)
3 postgraduate (*post-* : after)
4 intranet (*intra-* : inside/within)
5 disassembled (*dis-* : the opposite of)
6 illogical (*il-* : the opposite of)
7 mismanaged (*mis-* : badly/wrongly)
8 undervalued (*under-* : not enough)

REVIEW p51

AIMS

The aims of this section are to give students further practice in the skills learnt in this unit, and to give them the opportunity to review the work they have done. A further aim is to encourage students to apply what they have learnt to their other academic studies in English.

PROCEDURE

1 🔘 **6.8** Students read the instructions. Play the CD. Check the answers with the class. ⊙━ 1

2 🔘 **6.8** Students read the instructions. Point out that they are going to listen to the same interview again. Play the CD. Elicit the answers from some students. ⊙━ 2

3 Students read the instructions and do the task in pairs. Elicit answers as a class. ⊙━ 3

4 In their pairs, ask students to read the instructions and do the task. Monitor carefully. Ask one or two pairs to present their summaries to the class. Give feedback.

5 Students read the instructions and do the task. Check answers as a class. (You could also elicit where the other sentences would come in a presentation.) ⊙━ 5

EXTENSION ACTIVITY

Ask the students to list the skills they have learnt and practised in this unit. For example,
– establishing criteria
– critical thinking – detecting points of view and assumptions
– using an organization's or a company's website
– summarizing data from a table
– understanding and using prefixes

Put students in groups to discuss how to apply these skills to the work they do in their academic studies.

REVIEW Answer key p51

⊙━ 1

1 It gives grants of up to £50,000 to owners of historic buildings who need financial help for their buildings.
2 an important example of an architectural style/something significant happened in this place

⊙━ 2

1 Could you explain what it is exactly that the Preservation Committee does?
  How much would a typical grant be?
2 Could you give us an example?
  What do you mean by that?
3 Do you think that there is much public awareness of the historical buildings in our town?
4 Could you tell us the process you use to award this funding?
  Do you go into schools?

⊙━ 3
Possible answers

1 If you spend a lot of money, you get a better product.
2 Zippo cars are no good. A car shouldn't break down if it is two years old.
3 Buying shares when they are cheap is good. Mining companies' shares are low now but they will rise in value in the future.
4 Doubling the size of the airport will benefit passengers. Passengers want a bigger airport.
5 Cloudy with rain in most parts is bad weather. In Spain the weather is usually fine.

⊙━ 5

1, 3, 4, 6

7 Developments in architecture

LISTENING SKILLS Making inferences • Recognizing the plan of a talk • Mind mapping
SPEAKING SKILLS Critical thinking (7) Supporting a point of view • Preparing visuals
VOCABULARY DEVELOPMENT Learning subject-specific vocabulary

LISTENING Airports around the world pp52–53

AIMS

The aims of this section are to help students make inferences and recognize the plan of a talk. An additional aim is to practise mind mapping.

LEAD IN

- Focus the students' attention on the page. Ask them to identify the skill LISTENING, and the topic (*Airports around the world*).
- Put the students into pairs and ask them to talk about the last time they were in an airport. Ask:
  – *Was it a nice place to be?*
  – *Where was it and what can you remember about it?*

PROCEDURE

1 Students read the instructions and do the task in pairs. Get feedback from the class.

2 🔊 **7.1** Students read the instructions. Play the CD. Students listen and answer the questions. Elicit answers from some students. You could check subject-specific words such as 'hangars' and 'disembark'. ⚷ **2**

3 🔊 **7.2** Students read the instructions. Play the CD. Students do the task. Check the answers together. ⚷ **3**

4 🔊 **7.2** Students read the instructions. Point out that they are going to listen to the same podcast. Play the CD again. Students listen and complete the table. Check the information collected. ⚷ **4**

5 Students read the **STUDY SKILL** and the instructions. They do the task and discuss the answers in pairs. Go round and monitor. Check answers with the class. ⚷ **5**

6 🔊 **7.3** Students read the instructions. Point out that they are going to listen to extracts from the same podcast. Play the CD. Students do the task. Check the answers together. ⚷ **6**

7 Students read the instructions and discuss the questions in small groups. Monitor and encourage where necessary. Have a class discussion to share their answers. ⚷ **7**

8 Students read the instructions and discuss the points in their groups. Give them a time limit. Go round and monitor carefully, assisting where necessary. Ask each group to briefly present their airport ideas to the class.

LISTENING Answer key pp52–53

⚷ **2**

1 A surface for a plane to take off and land (runway).
2 Control towers, hangars, terminal buildings.
3 A terminal's main function is for passengers to board and disembark from aircraft.

⚷ **3**

1 Beijing Capital International Airport.
2 Changi Airport in Singapore.
3 Beijing: Terminal 3; Madrid: Terminal 4; Changi: Terminal 3.

⚷ **4**

1
Name: **Beijing Capital International Airport**
City: **Beijing, China**
Date completed: **2008**
Architects: **Foster and Partners**
Size: **1.3 million m^2**
Special features: **very efficient and sustainable, using natural light. From the air, looks like flying dragon, and inside uses traditional Chinese colours**

2
Name: **Madrid-Barajas Airport**
City: **Madrid, Spain**
Date completed: **2006**
Architects: **Richard Rogers**
Size: **760,000 m^2**
Special features: **use of natural light, wave-effect roof using bamboo, structural trees of graduated colour**

3
Name: **Changi Airport**
City: **Singapore**
Date completed: **2008**
Architects: **CPG Consultants**
Size: **430,000 m^2**
Special features: **'butterfly' roof to allow light in and keep out heat, vertical garden called 'The Green Wall' 300m across**

⚷ **5**

Possible answers
1 Steel is a strong material.
2 Terminal 3 is not big enough to cope with all the passengers.
3 Not all passengers buy their tickets, transfer their luggage and board their planes immediately; some passengers eat, shop or relax before boarding their planes.

⚷ **6**

1 Other, larger airports may be built in the future.
2 The airport was built as part of the preparation for the Beijing Olympics.
3 Dragons are an important part of Chinese culture.

⚷ **7**

Students' own answers.

Green skyscrapers pp54–55

1 Students read the instructions and answer the questions. Elicit the answers. 🔑 1

2 🔘 **7.4** Students read the **STUDY SKILL** and the instructions. Play the CD. Students listen and choose A, B or C. Check the answer together. It may be useful to look at the audioscript on p69 to clarify the phrases which indicate the order of the plan. 🔑 2

3 🔘 **7.5** Students read the **STUDY SKILL** and the instructions. Give them time to study the mind map on p55. Play the CD. Students do the tasks. Put them in pairs to check their answers. Elicit the definition. Draw the mind map on the board. Students could come up and write on it themselves. 🔑 3

4 Students read the instructions and answer the questions. Check the answers together. 🔑 4

5 🔘 **7.6** Students read the instructions. Clarify that they need to make two mind maps. Play the CD. They do the task. 🔑 5

6 Students read the instructions and do the task, using their notes from exercise 5. Put them in pairs to check their answers. Monitor carefully and clarify any problem answers as a class. 🔑 6

7 Put the students into pairs. They read the instructions and each student chooses one building to describe to the other. Monitor carefully and give constructive feedback.

EXTENSION ACTIVITY

Students listen to 🔘 **7.2** again and write down the plan for the podcast. Put the students in pairs to compare their plans. Play it again if necessary or direct students to the audio script on p68, then have a class discussion and write a plan on the board.

Possible plan

Introduction/Airport 1: basic facts, special design features
Airport 2: basic facts, special design features
Airport 3: basic facts, special design features
No conclusion because it's only part of a podcast.

LISTENING Answer key pp54–55

🔑 **1**

Students' own answers.

🔑 **2**

C

🔑 **3**

1 **Possible features:** a building which uses less water, optimizes energy efficiency, uses sustainable building materials, generates less waste, provides healthier spaces for occupants as compared to a conventional building.
2 The mind map should include the following points:

Water use:
– Recycle waste water

Features of green buildings:
– Energy efficiency:
  – Alternative sources of energy
  – Reduce energy used
– Sustainable building materials:
  – Natural
  – Recycled
– Waste management:
  – Reduce waste to a minimum

3 Students' own answers.

🔑 **4**

1 By using rain water or recycling waste water.
2 Solar power, wind turbines.
3 By using natural light where possible and materials which insulate the building.
4 Being able to continue using something without it having a negative effect on the environment.
5 Natural materials: stone, wood, paper, or recycled materials.
6 Water from the building can be used to water the gardens, and other waste can be composted or recycled.

🔑 **5**

Possible points

Pearl River Tower	**Bank of America Tower**
– Guangzhou, China	– Manhattan, New York, USA
– 309 metres high:	– 366 metres:
– 71 storeys	– 55 storeys
– Green features:	– spire = 78 metres
– Power source:	– Green features:
– wind turbines	– Energy:
– Radiant cooling:	– 50% less electricity
– pipes in ceiling	– natural lighting:
	– glass walls
	– gas-powered generator
	– Grey water

🔑 **6**

1 F: It's in Guangzhou.
2 F: It has 71 storeys.
3 T
4 T
5 F: It's cooling by the pipes in the ceiling.
6 F: It is 366 metres high. The spire is 78 metres high.
7 T
8 T
9 F: It will use 50% less electricity than ordinary buildings. '70%' refers to the percentage of the total power needs which will be provided for by the gas-powered generator.
10 T

SPEAKING Supporting your argument p56

AIMS

The aims of this section are to help students support their points of view and describe visuals.

LEAD IN

- Split the class in half and ask one half to brainstorm what they know about Hong Kong while the other half brainstorms what they know about Mumbai.
- Regroup the students in pairs to tell each other about their city.

PROCEDURE

1 Students look at the photos and read the instructions. Ask them to discuss the questions in pairs. Elicit ideas and write them on the board. **⊙ 1**

2 🔊 **7.7** Students read the **STUDY SKILL** and the instructions. Play the CD. Check the answers as a class. **⊙ 2**

3 Put the students in small groups. They read the instructions and each group divides into two teams to do the task. (At this stage they are only preparing their arguments.)

4 🔊 **7.8** Students read the instructions and the questions. Play the CD and students do the task. Elicit the answers.

Play the CD again for the students to focus on the expressions the speakers use to agree and disagree. Put them in pairs to check their answers. **⊙ 4**

5 Focus the students' attention on the Language Bank. In the same groups as exercise 3, students discuss whether skyscrapers are beneficial to cities. Monitor carefully.

6 Students read the instructions. Get feedback from the class, using the questions.

ADDITIONAL PHOTOCOPIABLE ACTIVITY

Speaking 7 Expressing points of view

Describing visuals p57

1 Students read the **STUDY SKILL** and the instructions. Put them in pairs to do the task. Elicit ideas from some students. **⊙ 1**

2 🔊 **7.9** Students read the instructions. Play the CD and students do the task. Elicit answers and students' reasons for their choices. **⊙ 2**

3 Students read the instructions and do the research task.

4 Students read the instructions and prepare short talks on their chosen building. Monitor carefully and assist where necessary.

5 Put the students in groups of four. They give their presentations and take notes on each other's talks. Give feedback.

EXTENSION ACTIVITY

Students listen again to 🔊 **7.8** and read the audio script on p70. They should underline phrases where the speakers introduce their opinions. Check them together.

Possible answers

it seems to me that …/ For one thing, …/ There is a danger that …/ I believe …/ I think…/ It will be… / Another thing is …/ I read that… / As I see it…/ There is a place for …

SPEAKING Answer key p56

⊙ 1

Students' own answers.

⊙ 2

1 She thinks they are essential for modern cities.
2 She gives examples and presents evidence.

⊙ 4

1 Introducing the Internet in schools.
2 Antonio and Carmen are against. Boris is for.
3 Point 1: children will waste time playing computer games and chatting online.
   Point 2: It will cost over a billion pounds.
   Point 3: What will happen to traditional teaching?
4 Agreeing:
   'I agree with' (Antonio).
   Disagreeing:
   'I see your point … but …'
   'That's not true.'
   'I don't think … '

SPEAKING Answer key p57

⊙ 1

Possible answers
A: There's too much information and the audience wouldn't be able to see it clearly.
B: This slide is not suitable because the layout should be clearer.
C: This is suitable because the information is clearly presented.
D: This slide is suitable because the photo is relevant to the talk.
E: This slide is suitable because the photo is relevant to the talk.
F: This slide is not suitable because the photo is not relevant to the talk.

⊙ 2

Possible answer
E, C, D

VOCABULARY DEVELOPMENT
Subject-specific vocabulary p58

AIMS
The aim of this section is to organize and learn subject-specific vocabulary.

LEAD IN
- Put students in groups of four or five and ask them to tell each other about their specific areas of study within their groups.

PROCEDURE
1 Students read the **STUDY SKILL** and the instructions, and do the task. Check the answers as a class. **⚿ 1**

2 Students read the instructions and categorize the vocabulary. Check the answers together. **⚿ 2**

3 Students read the instructions and do the task. Ask some students to give examples of their subject-specific vocabulary.

EXTENSION ACTIVITY
Ask the students to bring in a short text from their field of study. Put the students in pairs and tell them to swap texts. (Make sure the pairs include students with different subjects of study.) Ask students to underline vocabulary they believe is subject-specific. Tell them to discuss the underlined vocabulary together. If time, they could be put into different pairs to look at other texts.

VOCABULARY DEVELOPMENT Answer key p58

⚿ 1

1 dormer: subject-specific
  roof: general
2 geodesic dome: subject-specific
  structural: general
3 portico: subject-specific
4 tensile: subject-specific
  structures: general
  tension: subject-specific
  compression: subject-specific
  stability: general

⚿ 2

Medicine
mucous
cholesterol
pancreas
tumour

Architecture
buttress
lattice
rafter

Economics
monetarism
hedge funds
constructivism
tariff
tangible assets

REVIEW p59

AIMS

The aims of this section are to give students further practice in the skills learnt in this unit, and to give them the opportunity to review the work they have done. A further aim is to encourage students to apply what they have learnt to their other academic studies in English.

PROCEDURE

1 🔘 **7.10** Students read the instructions. Play the CD. Check the answers. 🔑 **1**

2 🔘 **7.10** Students read the instructions. Play the CD again. Students do the task. Elicit the answers and ask the reasons for their answers. 🔑 **2**

3 Put the students into pairs. They read the instructions and take a role each. Students look at the table, then do the discussion task. Monitor carefully. Refer them to the Language Bank on p56 if necessary.

4 Students read the instructions and complete the task. Check the answers. 🔑 **4**

5 Students read the instructions and complete the task. Elicit the answers from the class. 🔑 **5**

EXTENSION ACTIVITY

Ask the students to list the skills they have learnt and practised in this unit. For example,
– recognizing the plan of a talk
– mind-mapping
– how to support your point of view
– preparing visuals
– learning subject-specific vocabulary

Put students in groups to discuss how to apply these skills to the work they do in their academic studies.

REVIEW Answer key p59

🔑 1

Possible points for the mind map:

Style
– influenced by nature + naturally-occurring figures
– fluid, evolving shapes, curved lines
– fits in well in its environment
– good for countryside + places of natural beauty

Architects
– Gaudí
– Frank Lloyd Wright

Buildings
– Casa Milà (Barcelona) looks like cliff face + caves
– Fallingwater (USA)

🔑 2

– Most modern architecture uses flat shapes and straight lines.
– Antoni Gaudí wanted people to feel like they were entering a cave when they entered Casa Milà.
– Fallingwater does not look out of place.

🔑 4

1 d   2 e   3 c   4 b   5 a

🔑 5

1 subsidiaries
2 ecosystem
3 lintel
4 neurological
5 microprocessors

8 The sports industry

LISTENING SKILLS Recognizing the structure of an interview • Reviewing and organizing notes
RESEARCH Using keywords in research
SPEAKING SKILLS Successful interviews • Presentations (6) Logical organization • Establishing rapport
VOCABULARY DEVELOPMENT Word families

LISTENING Sports sponsorship pp60–61

AIMS

The aims of this section are to help students recognize the structure of an interview and to give students practice in reviewing and organizing their notes.

LEAD IN

• Focus the students' attention on the page. Ask them to identify the skill LISTENING, and the topic (*Sports sponsorship*).
• Put the students into pairs and ask them to write a definition of the word 'sponsorship'. Elicit ideas and write the best definition on the board.

PROCEDURE

1 Students read the instructions, look at the photos and do the task. Get feedback from the class. **⊶ 1**

2 Students read the instructions and complete the text. Elicit the answers. **⊶ 2**

3 Students read the instructions and discuss the questions in pairs. Have a class discussion based on their ideas.

4 🔊 **8.1** Students read the instructions. Play the CD. Students listen and do the task. Check the answers together. **⊶ 4**

5 🔊 **8.2** Students read the **STUDY SKILL** and the instructions. Play the CD. Students listen and do the task. Elicit answers to check together. **⊶ 5**

6 🔊 **8.2** Students read the instructions. Point out that they are going to listen to the same interview again. Play the CD. Students do the task. Check the answers together. **⊶ 6**

7 🔊 **8.3** Students read the instructions. Play the CD.

8 Have a class discussion about the advantages and disadvantages of sports sponsorship based on the students' lists from exercise 7. Encourage the students to give their opinions and back them up wherever possible. **⊶ 8**

ADDITIONAL PHOTOCOPIABLE ACTIVITY

Speaking 8 Information gap

LISTENING Answer key pp60–61

⊶ 1
1 Emirates logo (= airline) and the Arsenal logo (= football club) – football
2 Shell, Santander, Ferrari – Formula One racing
3 Npower (pronounced 'en'-power = gas and electricity supply company) – cricket
4 Nike – tennis

⊶ 2
1 business
2 funds
3 organization
4 which
5 return
6 sponsorship

⊶ 4
1 In the 1930s in the USA.
2 Through sponsorship in the 2010 World Cup.
3 Individuals: Cristiano Ronaldo, the spectator
Sports and companies: baseball, FIFA (football)
Sponsors: Visa, Nike, Pepsi Cola
TV companies

⊶ 5
3 sports which attract sponsorship
5 disadvantages of sponsorship
6 the future of sports sponsorship
1 definition of sports sponsorship
4 advantages of sponsorship
2 what companies get out of sponsorship

⊶ 6
1 T
2 F: Sponsorship is really marketing.
3 F: Football and F1 racing attract the most sponsorship internationally.
4 F: Standards have been raised.
5 F: Sponsors often concentrate on the big sports.
6 T
7 F: He can see both positive and negative aspects.

⊶ 8
Advantages
Money for improved facilities.
TV deals mean more people can see sports.
Raised standards – teams with more money attract better players.
Individual sportsmen and women can focus on their sport.

Disadvantages
People don't like seeing advertising everywhere.
Sponsors neglect smaller sports.
Some sponsors want to change the times that sports are played.
Some sponsors want to change the rules of sports – which may change the game too much.
Some sports may become dependent on sponsorship.

The science of sport pp61–62

1 Students read the instructions, look at the photos, and answer the questions. Elicit their ideas.

2 Students read the instructions and do the discussion task in small groups. Go round and monitor. Ask one or two students to talk to the class.

3 🔊 **8.4** Students read the instructions. Play the CD. Students take notes. Elicit the answers to the questions. You may need to write the key words on the board to clarify spelling. ⊶ 3

4 🔊 **8.5** Students read the instructions. Play the CD. They take notes using a mind map or linear notes.

5 🔊 **8.6** Students read the instructions. Play the CD. They do the task.

6 Students read the instructions and do the task, using their notes. Put them in pairs to check their answers. Monitor carefully and clarify any problem answers as a class. ⊶ 6

7 Students read the **STUDY SKILL** and the instructions and discuss the questions. Monitor carefully and get feedback from the class. ⊶ 7

8 Students read the instructions and review their notes from exercises 3, 4 and 5. Go round and monitor. Check they are using the techniques from the Study Skill box.

EXTENSION ACTIVITY

Students listen to 🔊 **8.5** again and write down the signal expressions which help them recognize the structure of the talk. You could ask them to listen one more time and read the audio script on p71 in order to check their answers.

Possible answers

Let's begin with…/ Now a second important factor is …/ The next factor …/ So that's just one example of …/ Let's move on to …/ A final factor…

LISTENING Answer key pp61–62

⊶ 3

1 What makes a champion.
2 Physiology, nutrition, sports technology, performance analysis, psychology.

⊶ 6

1 The study of how an athlete's body works.
2 Fats, carbohydrates, proteins.
3 Carbohydrates.
4 Wood.
5 Carbon fibre, fibreglass and metals such as titanium.
6 Evaluating performance looking at statistical information and video records.
7 Managing emotions and minimizing the psychological effects of injury and poor performance.
8 Top athletes become champions through training and exercising hard. There are a number of ways in which science can also help top hard-working athletes become champions.

⊶ 7

Possible answers
1 The notes are just a list of points, with many missing points. They could be improved by showing the relationship between the information.
2 Sports physiology – functioning of the body:
   • we can help athletes – running, jumping
   • we learn how the body works
   Nutrition – food and drink:
   • three classes:
      carbohydrates
      fats
      proteins
   Sports technology – sports equipment
   • tennis racquet
   • football boots

RESEARCH Keywords p63

AIMS

The aim of this section is to help students use keywords effectively in their research.

LEAD IN

- Put students in pairs to discuss what 'keywords' are and where and how we might use them. Elicit ideas.

PROCEDURE

1 Students read the **STUDY SKILL** and the instructions, and do the task. Check the answers together. 🔑 1

2 Students read the instructions and do the task in groups of four. Make sure each student chooses a different title from exercise 1. Give them a time limit to do their research. Remind them to give a reference for their sources and refer them back to the Study Skill on p15 if necessary. Monitor, assist and encourage the students.

3 Students read the instructions and do the task. Monitor carefully.

4 Students read the instructions and choose a company to research. Give them a time limit, monitor and assist. Check the completed tables yourself as far as possible, or, in a large class, regroup the students so that they can check their tables with classmates who researched the same company.

EXTENSION ACTIVITY

Students write lists of useful keywords for their own fields of study. If there is time, they could research an aspect of their own studies and find out whether these keywords worked successfully or not.

RESEARCH Answer key p63

🔑 1

1 The **effects** of **global warming** on the **ice caps** of the **polar** regions.
2 The **costs** of **nuclear power** compared to other sources of **renewable energy**.
3 The **relationship** between **academic performance** and **physical fitness** amongst **school children**.
4 The role of **continental drift** in the **formation** of the **Himalayan mountain range**.

SPEAKING Interviewing p64

AIMS

The aim of this section is to help students conduct effective interviews and organize their talks logically. An additional aim is to help students establish rapport with their audience.

LEAD IN

- Ask the students to remember the last interview they experienced. Put them into pairs to discuss their memories. Ask:
  – *Was it a good or bad interview? Why?*
- Have a class discussion and write any interesting ideas on the board.

PROCEDURE

1 Students read the instructions and discuss the questions in pairs. Elicit ideas from some students.

2 ⊙ **8.7** Students read the instructions. Play the CD. Students do the task. Elicit answers from the class. ⊙⌐ **2**

3 Students read the **STUDY SKILL** and the instructions. They add to their lists. Go round and monitor.

4 In pairs, students read the instructions and discuss the interview questions. Elicit the answers and the reasons behind them. ⊙⌐ **4**

5 In the same pairs as before, students read the instructions and prepare to do the task. Give them a time limit if necessary. They role play the interviews together. Invite one or two pairs to do their role play for the class.

Logical organization p65

1 Students read the instructions and discuss the questions in pairs. Check students' ideas as a class.

2 ⊙ **8.8** Students read the **STUDY SKILL** and the instructions. Play the CD and students do the task. Check the answers as a class. ⊙⌐ **2**

3 Students read the instructions and choose a topic. In pairs, they discuss how they would divide the talk. Go round and monitor.

4 ⊙ **8.8** Students read the **STUDY SKILL** and the instructions. Focus their attention on the Language Bank. Play the CD again. They do the task. Check the answers together. ⊙⌐ **4**

5 Students read the instructions, choose a topic, and plan a short presentation. Give a time limit, monitor carefully and assist where necessary. Students give their presentations to the class.

EXTENSION ACTIVITY

Put students in pairs. Tell them that they are going to interview each other about the subject of their studies. First of all, they need to prepare, so give them 15 minutes to mingle and find out as much as they can about their partner and what he/she studies from their classmates. They then have 10 minutes to prepare good interview questions. Finally, they take it in turns to conduct the interviews. Monitor the interviews carefully. After they have done the task, encourage class discussion about how successful the questions were, whether follow-up questions were asked and how well they worked, and any general feedback about the interview process.

SPEAKING Answer key p64

⊙⌐ **2**

Possible answers

Interview B is better. The interviewer is much better prepared, introduces himself, has clearly planned questions, and has accurate information about the interviewee's background.

Interview A: The interviewer is not well prepared. He gets the interviewee's name wrong, and asks short, boring questions.

⊙⌐ **4**

1 Not good – it's a closed question – Yes/No.
2 Good – it will get information.
3 Good – asking for factual information.
4 Good – it will get most of the same information as question 3, also the interviewee's opinion.
5 Not good – Yes/No doesn't get the names of companies.
6 Good for clarification.
7 Not good – Yes/No.
8 Good – it will get information and opinion.

SPEAKING Answer key p65

⊙⌐ **2**

1 The very first tennis racquets, the first metal racquets, modern racquets, the future of tennis racquets.
2 Listing factors.

⊙⌐ **4**

He establishes a rapport with the audience by:
– asking questions to include the audience's experience: 'How many people here play tennis?', 'How many people like to watch tennis on TV?'
– asking straight questions: 'What about the future of tennis racquets?', 'How far can science go in producing the perfect racquet?'

VOCABULARY DEVELOPMENT Word families p66

AIMS
The aim of this section is to improve students' knowledge and understanding of word families.

LEAD IN
- Write the term 'word families' on the board. Elicit what the students understand this to mean. Clarify and elicit the different parts of speech (*verb, noun, adjective, adverb*).

PROCEDURE
1 Students read the **STUDY SKILL** and the instructions, and complete the table. Elicit the answers and write them on the board. **⊶1**

2 Students read the instructions and complete the task. Draw the table on the board and invite students to come up and fill in the spaces. **⊶2**

3 Students read the instructions and complete the sentences. Elicit the answers from the students. **⊶3**

EXTENSION ACTIVITY
Give students a slip of paper and ask them to draw four columns on it. Ask them to write one word on it that they think has a word family they could find in a dictionary. They should write this word in the column corresponding to the correct part of speech, as in exercise 2. Repeat this process twice so that each student has put one word on three slips of paper in total.

Put the slips of paper in a hat or bag. Each student selects three slips of paper at random and works out the members of the word families, using a dictionary if necessary. Students write the word families in the columns as in exercise 2. Monitor carefully. All the slips of paper can be made into a poster or display. Draw attention to common word endings for different parts of speech.

VOCABULARY DEVELOPMENT Answer key p66

⊶1

verb	noun	adjective	adverb
succeed	success	successful	successfully

⊶2

verb	noun	adjective	adverb
benefit	**benefit**	**beneficial**	beneficially
analyze	**analysis**	analytical	**analytically**
—	technology	**technological**	**technologically**
dramatize	drama	**dramatic**	**dramatically**
relax	**relaxation**	relaxing/relaxed	—
perform	performer	performing	—

⊶3

1 beneficial
2 performance
3 relax
4 analytically
5 dramatically
6 technological

REVIEW p67

AIMS

The aims of this section are to give students further practice in the skills learnt in this unit, and to give them the opportunity to review the work they have done. A further aim is to encourage students to apply what they have learnt to their other academic studies in English.

PROCEDURE

1 🔘 **8.9** Students read the instructions. Play the CD and students order the points. Check the answers. 🔑 **1**

2 🔘 **8.9** Students read the instructions and study the notes. Play the CD again and students do the task. Elicit answers from the class. 🔑 **2**

3 Students read the instructions and do the task. Monitor carefully. You could put the students in pairs to compare their questions or just elicit questions from some students. 🔑 **3**

4 Students read the instructions and look at the two plans for talks. Ask them to number the headings in a logical order. Check the answers together. 🔑 **4**

5 Students read the instructions and complete the sentences individually. Put students in pairs to compare answers. Clarify any answers where they do not agree. 🔑 **5**

EXTENSION ACTIVITY

Ask the students to list the skills they have learnt and practised in this unit. For example,
– recognizing the structure of an interview
– using keywords in research
– conducting successful interviews
– organizing presentations logically
– learning about word families

Put students in groups to discuss how to apply these skills to the work they do in their academic studies.

REVIEW Answer key p67

🔑 1

1 Benefits of sponsorship for companies
2 Deciding who to sponsor
   (Benefits of sponsorship for athletes – not mentioned)
3 Sponsoring teams
4 Risks involved in sponsorship

🔑 2

Sponsorship:
  – endorse products
  – publicity
Individuals:
  – successful
  – image
  – good-looking
  – charisma
Teams:
  – benefits
Risks:
  – scandal

🔑 3

Possible answers
1 What do you think of distance learning?
2 Why would you choose or not choose to study a course by distance?
3 What kind of people is distance learning suitable for?
4 Which subjects can't be studied by distance?
5 What are the disadvantages to distance learning?

🔑 4

1 **Internet addiction**
Introduction
  5 Will these solutions work?
  3 Why is it a problem?
  1 What is Internet addiction? Definition
  2 How many people are affected?
  4 Possible solutions
Conclusion

2 **The development of computers**
Introduction
  3 Digital computers
  5 Where do we go from here?
  1 Desktop calculators
  4 Current computers
  2 Analogue computers
Conclusion

🔑 5

1 sponsored
2 commercialization
3 successful
4 Success
5 motivate

LISTENING SKILLS   Interpreting data in maps • Recognizing tentative language • Recognizing lecture styles
• Getting the most out of visuals
SPEAKING SKILLS   Describing results in a presentation • Analyzing data critically • Presenting a survey report
VOCABULARY DEVELOPMENT   Recognizing multiple meanings

LISTENING   Trends in world population pp68–69

AIMS
The aims of this section are to help students interpret data in maps and to give students practice in recognizing tentative language and lecture styles.

LEAD IN
• Focus the students' attention on the page. Ask them to identify the skill LISTENING, and the topic (*Trends in world population*).
• Put the students into pairs and ask them to discuss whether they think the population in their country is increasing or decreasing, together with any possible reasons for this trend.

PROCEDURE
1 Students read the instructions and discuss the questions in small groups. Get feedback from the whole class. **⌐1**

2 Students read the **STUDY SKILL** and the instructions. In their groups, they look at the map and key and discuss the questions. Elicit the answers. **⌐2**

3 🔊 **9.1** Students read the instructions. Play the CD. Students listen and do the task. Check the answers together. **⌐3**

4 🔊 **9.1** Students read the instructions and the statements. Play the CD again. Students listen and do the task. Elicit answers to check together. **⌐4**

5 🔊 **9.2** Students read the **STUDY SKILL**. Draw their attention to the words 'tentative', 'not certain' and 'cautious'. Students then read the instructions, listen, and make a note of the language used. Check the answers as a class. **⌐5**

6 Students read the instructions and discuss the problems in small groups, trying to find solutions. Get feedback from the whole class. **⌐6**

LISTENING   Answer key pp68–69

⌐1
Student's own answers.

⌐2
1 High growth: Sub-Saharan Africa and parts of the Middle East
   Low growth: Europe, North America, East Asia
2 These countries are located around the equator.
3 These countries have cooler climates.
4 Exceptions: Tunisia has a lower birth rate than the countries it borders.
5 Wealth, migration, health and healthcare – epidemics/famine and other disasters, cultural norms.

⌐3
1 The world population is rising but at a slower rate.
2 There is wide variation from region to region.
3 Many factors: births/deaths, migration, standard of healthcare, diseases/wars/natural disasters and in some regions/countries people just want smaller families.
4 To plan healthcare, education, energy consumption, support for the elderly.
5 The overall birth rate is falling so if this continues the world population will eventually fall (possibly as early as 2040).

⌐4
1 T
2 F: to between 8 and 10.5 billion
3 F: lower
4 T
5 F: only births and deaths
6 F: also take into account migration
7 T
8 T

⌐5
1 Some regions **tend to** have a very high growth rate ...
2 However, people don't stay at home – **for one reason or another**, **a significant number of** people move to other countries.
3 ... Yemen, the population growth rates **tend to be** high. That is **mainly** due to a high birth rate.
4 There are **probably** many reasons for that – but **it seems that** people **generally** want to have smaller families.
5 Another factor **could be** that, **on the whole**, immigrants to these countries **are likely to** have more children.
6 ... as families, **on average**, **seem to** want fewer children.
7 ... the world population **is likely to** fall, **perhaps** as early as 2040.

⌐6
Students' own ideas.

Is life getting better? pp70–71

1 Students read the instructions and discuss the questions in pairs. 🔑1

2 Students read the instructions and do the questionnaire. Ask them to compare scores in pairs.

3 Students read the instructions and do the brainstorming task in small groups. Go round and monitor. Encourage whole class discussion.

4 In their groups, students read the instructions and discuss the terms in the box, using dictionaries or reference sources if necessary. Elicit some ideas (though the students will find out the true definitions in the next exercise.)

5 💿 9.3 Students read the **STUDY SKILL** and the instructions. Play the CD. Students do the task. Check the answers together. 🔑5

6 💿 9.4 Students read the **STUDY SKILL** and the instructions. Play the CD. Students complete the information on the visuals. Check the answers. 🔑6

7 💿 9.4 Students read the instructions. Play the CD again. Students answer the questions. Elicit the answers from the class. 🔑7

8 Students read the instructions. Put them into groups of three, and ask each student to choose one graph. Give them a time limit to study their graphs and prepare to describe them, following the instructions. Students present their graph to their group. Monitor carefully and get class feedback at the end to highlight successes and difficulties they had in doing the task.

EXTENSION ACTIVITY

Ask students to prepare a short talk about their country, entitled 'The Gross Domestic Happiness of …'. They can include the three HDI dimensions – health, knowledge and standard of living – plus any dimensions they personally feel are important to human happiness. They can use just their own ideas or include information from the website http://hdr.undp.org/en/statistics (if available). Ask them to decide whether their talk will be formal or informal and tell them to use tentative language in their talk. When ready, they can present their talks to the class. The class should take notes and ask questions. Give constructive feedback.

LISTENING Answer key pp70–71

🔑1

Students' own ideas.

🔑5

1 HDI: Human Development Index is a common measure of the quality of life.
2 Structure: HDI, global picture of quality of life, trends over recent years, opponents of HDI, and alternative measures of quality of life.
3 Informal style – the speaker uses direct questions, humour, not academic language, e.g. 'I'll start off by looking at...', 'So let's get going.'

🔑6

1 **HDI by country for year 2010**
   1 Norway   0.938
   2 **Australia**   **0.937**
   3 **New Zealand**   **0.907**

2 **HDI trends**
   (from top to bottom)
   – **OECD states**
   – **Eastern Europe**
   – Latin America and the Caribbean
   – East Asia
   – **Arab states**
   – **South Asia**
   – Sub-Saharan Africa

🔑7

1 1990.
2 Health (measured by life expectancy), knowledge (measured by years of schooling), standard of living (measured by income).
3 0.8 and above.
4 Improvement in HDI will continue in all regions of the world
5 No ecological consideration, the scale is too small and gives little room for improvement, no spiritual or moral component.
6 Measuring the happiness of a country, 'Gross Domestic Happiness'.

SPEAKING Presenting results p72

AIMS

The aims of this section are to help students present results effectively and analyze data critically. An additional aim is to help students present a survey report with the correct structure.

LEAD IN

- Put students into pairs. Write on the board the terms, 'pie chart', 'graph', and 'bar chart', and ask the students to discuss what kind of data is best represented by each kind of chart. (*Possible answers: pie chart: percentages of a whole; graph: where two factors need to be considered, e.g. trends over time; bar chart: categories of the same data, e.g. population in different countries at a given point in time.*)
- Have a whole class discussion.

PROCEDURE

1 Students read the instructions and look at the visuals. They then discuss the questions in pairs. Elicit answers from some students. **🔑 1**

2 **9.5** Students read the **STUDY SKILL** and the instructions. Play the CD. Students do the task and compare their answers in pairs. Clarify as a class, if necessary. **🔑 2**

3 **9.6** Students read the **STUDY SKILL** and the instructions. Highlight the word 'misrepresent' and check the meaning. Play the CD. Students do the task. Elicit answers. **🔑 3**

4 Put students into groups of four. Ask them to read the instructions and discuss the bar chart. Monitor carefully.

ADDITIONAL PHOTOCOPIABLE ACTIVITY

Speaking 9 Analyzing data

Discussing a survey report p73

1 Students read the **STUDY SKILL** and the instructions. Ask them to discuss the content of the survey report in pairs. Elicit ideas from the class.

2 **9.7** Students read the **STUDY SKILL** and the instructions. Play the CD and students do the task. Check the answers. **🔑 2**

3 **9.7** Students read the instructions. Play the CD again. Check the answers as a class. **🔑 3**

4 Students read the instructions and the information. Ask them to follow points 1–3 to prepare their presentations. Monitor this process carefully and assist where necessary. Give clear time limits.

5 Students give their presentations to the class. Get whole class feedback, giving constructive criticism.

EXTENSION ACTIVITY

Put students in pairs. Ask them to look again at the charts on p72. Tell each student to choose one chart and describe it to their partner. They should intentionally misrepresent some of the data. Their partner needs to listen carefully in order to spot which data is misrepresented and in what way.

SPEAKING Answer key p72

🔑 1

1 Student attendance at Park Lane Language school 2001–2010, and the use of students' free time during the semester and the holidays.
2–4 Students' own answers.

🔑 2

Speaker 1 makes sure the audience focuses on the visual: 'This chart shows...'.
He focuses on important information: 'Overall'.
He gives possible reasons: 'This might have been due to', and uses tentative language.

Speaker 2 makes sure the audience focuses on the visual: 'If you look at this table'. She gives possible reasons using tentative language: 'it is likely', 'seem to indicate'.

🔑 3

1 The speaker infers a casual relationship without providing evidence.
2 This speaker also infers a casual relationship without providing evidence.
3 The speaker uses a very small sample and then overgeneralizes.
4 The speaker draws a false conclusion.

SPEAKING Answer key p73

🔑 2

1 The attitude of people shopping in malls to smoking in malls.
2 A Method
  B Conclusion
  C Introduction
  D Results

🔑 3

A 1 It was a random sample.
  2 Because during the week there wouldn't be many young people and they wanted a range of ages.
B 1 About 65%.
  2 Set smoking areas aside.
C 1 Most of them.
  2 It is thought to be a cause of respiratory diseases and cancer and is especially dangerous for small children
D 1 A pie chart and a table.
  2 About 25%.

VOCABULARY DEVELOPMENT Multiple meanings p74

AIMS

The aim of this section is to improve students' knowledge and understanding of words with multiple meanings.

LEAD IN

- Write the words 'change', 'bank', 'wood', 'book' on the board and elicit what they have in common (*they all have more than one meaning*).
- Put students into pairs to discuss the different meanings of these words.

PROCEDURE

1 Students read the **STUDY SKILL** and the instructions, and do the task. Elicit the answers. ⊙⌐ 1

2 Students read the instructions and complete the task. Check the answers together. ⊙⌐ 2

3 Students read the instructions and do the task. Monitor carefully. Get feedback from the class, eliciting example sentences. ⊙⌐ 3

EXTENSION ACTIVITY

Ask students to find a text from their own field of study and read it carefully, looking for words which could have more than one meaning. Each time they think they have found one such word, they should look it up in a dictionary and make a record of the different meanings.

VOCABULARY DEVELOPMENT Answer key p74

⊙⌐ 1

1 sector: part of the business activity of a country
2 trade: a job for which you need a special skill
3 faculty: one department in a university, college, etc.

⊙⌐ 2

1 comparative part, share of a whole
2 to usually do or be something
3 a programme designed to do a particular job
4 the way that something is used, the amount that something is used
5 easy to get, use or understand

⊙⌐ 3

Students' own answers.

REVIEW p75

AIMS

The aims of this section are to give students further practice in the skills learnt in this unit, and to give them the opportunity to review the work they have done. A further aim is to encourage students to apply what they have learnt to their other academic studies in English.

PROCEDURE

1 🔊 **9.8** Students read the instructions and study the maps. Play the CD. Elicit the answer from one student. 🔑 **1**

2 Students read the instructions and the statements, and do the task. Elicit the answers as a class. 🔑 **2**

3 🔊 **9.9** Students read the instructions. Play the CD. Students correct the information. Check the answers together. 🔑 **3**

4 Students read the instructions and look at the survey findings. Ask them to plan a presentation in pairs. Refer them back to the Study Skill boxes on pp71–72, if necessary. Give a time limit. Invite some students to give their presentations. Give constructive criticism.

EXTENSION ACTIVITY

Ask the students to list the skills they have learnt and practised in this unit. For example,
– interpreting data in maps
– recognizing and using tentative language
– describing results in a presentation
– analyzing data critically
– recognizing multiple meanings

Put students in groups to discuss how to apply these skills to the work they do in their academic studies.

REVIEW   Answer key   p75

🔑 **1**

Map B.

🔑 **2**

Possible answers

1 It is likely that the price of oil will rise in the next few months. / The price of oil will probably/is likely to rise in the next few months.
2 It seems that people in Andorra tend to live much longer than people in Russia.
3 ... This was probably due to the recession in the UK.
4 In general, students spend/tend to spend more time in the library...
5 The survey shows that, generally speaking, many/most young people eat fast food...
6 Eating fast food may cause/is likely to cause obesity ...

🔑 **3**

1 Human **Poverty** Index
  • Developed by United **Nations**
  • Is used to measure **developed** countries
2 **Sweden**
  • People lacking **functional literacy skills** 7.5
  • Long-term unemployment **1.1**

10 Technological advances

LISTENING SKILLS Critical listening • Dealing with fast speech • Active listening: asking questions
• Pronunciation: homophones
SPEAKING SKILLS Recognizing an opposing view • Presentations (7) Delivery
VOCABULARY DEVELOPMENT Register (formal and informal)

LISTENING The end of books? pp76–77

AIMS
The aims of this section are to help students practise critical listening and deal with fast speech. Additional aims are to help students improve their techniques for asking questions and their awareness of homophones.

LEAD IN
• Focus the students' attention on the page. Ask them to identify the skill LISTENING, and the topic (*The end of books?*).
• Put the students into pairs and ask them to find out as much as possible about their partners' reading habits, e.g. *Does he/she read most for study or pleasure? What does he/she read? What percentage of his/her reading is book-based?*
• Monitor then conduct a class discussion on this topic.

PROCEDURE
1 Students read the instructions and do the task in pairs. Get feedback from the class.

2 Students read the instructions and discuss the questions in small groups. They should work together to brainstorm the answers and complete the table, using the Language Bank to give opinions. Elicit the students' ideas and write some on the board.

3 ⊚ 10.1 Students read the instructions. Play the CD. Students listen and do the task. Check the answers together. ⊙ 3

4 ⊚ 10.2 Students read the **STUDY SKILL** and the instructions. Play the CD. Students listen and answer the questions. Put them in small groups to compare answers. Monitor and elicit answers to check together if necessary. ⊙ 4

5 ⊚ 10.2 Students read the instructions and the questions. Play the CD again. Check the answers as a class. ⊙ 5

6 Students read the instructions and do the matching task. Elicit answers from some students. ⊙ 6

7 Students read the instructions and discuss the conclusions and the questions. Have a class feedback session on their views.

LISTENING Answer key pp76–77

⊙ 3
1 They have just launched a new e-book service.
2 Videos, pictures, music, computer games.
3 Does everyone really gain from e-publishing?
4 Jamie Lee, the Managing Director of Chance Publishing.

⊙ 4
1 He thinks e-books are useful and that the reading experience has been made more rewarding and interesting by having media content included. He says e-books will take over a substantial sector of the publishing business.
2 He says it's easier to carry and store books on an e-reader. Also e-screens are better now and easier to read.
3 He talks about sales figures but doesn't give any data.
4 Publishers and authors should embrace e-publishing as it's a new market and will bring a new group of people back to reading.
5 Students' own evaluation.

⊙ 5
1 New books from their own authors and multi-media extras.
2 Because you can have pictures, a short video or an audio soundtrack too.
3 No, he says some people will still prefer the traditional book.
4 An e-reader saves space and makes it easy to carry 200 books around, travel or move house.
5 The glare is reduced in modern e-readers and many have e-ink which reduces glare.
6 Because they tried to stop people downloading music instead of embracing the new market.
7 They should welcome it.
8 The market will improve. It has been in decline but e-publishing will bring new readers back to reading.

⊙ 6
1 d   2 b   3 a   4 c

Technology of the future pp78–79

1 Students read the instructions and do the task in pairs.

2 Students read the instructions and discuss the terms in pairs. Go round and monitor. Encourage some students to give their ideas to the class.

3 🎧 **10.3** Students read the instructions. Play the CD. Students answer the questions. Check the answers together. 🔑 **3**

4 🎧 **10.4** Students read the **STUDY SKILL** and the instructions. (You could highlight that they should listen for the stressed words.) Play the CD. They do the underlining task. Check the answers. It would be useful to have the extracts projected on the board so you can underline the words. 🔑 **4**

5 Students read the **STUDY SKILL** and the instructions, and do the task. Check the answers together. 🔑 **5**

6 🎧 **10.5** Students read the instructions. Play the CD. They take notes.

7 🎧 **10.5** Students read the instructions and do the task. Play the CD again, pausing where appropriate to check the answers. 🔑 **7**

8 Students read the instructions and write five questions. Monitor carefully. Put the students into pairs to compare their questions and elicit some to write on the board.

9 🎧 **10.6** Students read the **STUDY SKILL** and the instructions. Play the CD. They do the task. Check the answers together. 🔑 **9**

EXTENSION ACTIVITY

Put the students into pairs. Ask them to brainstorm (secretly!) other sets of homophones. Monitor and give them ideas if necessary.

They should then write pairs of sentences, leaving gaps where the homophone words would be, similar to the sentences in exercise 9. Finally, student pairs swap and try to complete each other's sentences.

LISTENING Answer key pp78–79

🔑 3

1 By asking if the technology is likely to change the world.
2 Better bio-fuels, more efficient solar cells, green concrete.
3 No, some are local: 3D screens on mobile devices, new apps for cloud computing, social television.
4 New ways to implant medical electronics.

🔑 4

1 See example answer.
2 Some of these **changes** are on the **largest** possible **scale**: **better bio-fuels**, **more efficient solar cells** and **green concrete** all **aim** to **tackle global warming** in the years ahead.
3 Other **changes** are more **local** and involve how we **use technology**: for example, **3D screens** on **mobile devices**, new **applications** for **cloud computing** and **social television**.
4 What I'd like to do in **today's lecture**, the last in this **semester** on **Technology**, is to **briefly review five** of the **selected technologies** – **new** technologies that may become **important** in the **near future**.
5 The **five examples** we have selected come from **five different fields** – from **communication**, **construction**, **medicine**, **science** and lastly the **media**.

🔑 5

1 opinion
2 repetition
3 clarification
4 further information

🔑 7

1 T
2 F: Biofuels come from crops such as corn. Solar fuels would come from microbes.
3 T
4 T
5 T
6 F: They biodegrade so don't need to be removed.
7 F: It is declining.
8 T

🔑 9

1 week
2 weak
3 weight
4 wait
5 steel
6 steal
7 principal
8 principle
9 site
10 sight

SPEAKING Giving and supporting opinions p80

AIMS

The aims of this section are to help students recognize an opposing view and to help them improve the delivery of their presentations.

LEAD IN

- Write the following situation on the board:
  You are discussing something with a friend and find that they have a very different point of view.
  Do you a) change the subject b) try to change their mind c) agree to disagree d) seriously consider their arguments e) change your mind?
- Put the students into pairs to discuss the situation, and then have a class discussion.

PROCEDURE

1 Students read the instructions and discuss their preference in pairs. Invite some students to talk about their choice.

2 🔊 **10.7** Students read the **STUDY SKILL** and the instructions. Play the CD. Students do the task. Check the answers together. ⚬⌐ 2

3 Students read the instructions and the statements. Refer them to the Language Bank. Monitor while they do the task and elicit ideas to write on the board. ⚬⌐ 3

4 Put the students into groups. Ask them to read the instructions and choose one topic each. Students research their topic and prepare to give their opinion in a presentation. Give them a time limit for this presentation stage and monitor carefully.

5 Students give two-minute presentations to the members of their group. Others in the group may ask questions. Get feedback from the groups and give constructive criticism.

ADDITIONAL PHOTOCOPIABLE ACTIVITY

Speaking 10 Building an argument

Giving a presentation on new technology p81

1 Students read the instructions and discuss the structure of the presentation in pairs. Elicit ideas.

2 🔊 **10.8** Students read the **STUDY SKILL** and the instructions. Play the CD and students do the task. Put them in pairs to discuss their answers. Check ideas together as a class ⚬⌐ 2

3 Students read the instructions and do the task. Check the answers as a class. ⚬⌐ 3

4 Students read the instructions and decide on the topic of their presentation in pairs. Draw their attention to the checklist and give them a time limit to prepare their presentation, including visuals. Monitor carefully.

5 Students give their presentations to the class. Encourage note-taking, questions and constructive criticism, especially regarding delivery (looking again at the Study Skill box on p81 if necessary).

EXTENSION ACTIVITY

Put students in small groups. Give them contentious topics to discuss and ask them to talk together, acknowledging opposing views and backing up their own opinions using the Language Bank on p80 if necessary.

Possible topics:

All school-age children should be given mobile phones./Every working person should give 10% of their income to charity./Women are better at communicating than men./Testing drugs on animals is necessary.

SPEAKING Answer key p80

⚬⌐ 2

1 Speaker B.
2 He backs up his opinions, but he also acknowledges the other side.
3 It's very basic. She gives opinions without backing them up and does not acknowledge that there are other arguments.

⚬⌐ 3

Possible answers

1 Although I admit that it may cost the taxpayer money, I believe public transport should be free in cities.
2 I agree that childhood is a time for playing and having fun. Nevertheless, I feel that children should be given jobs to do in the home.
3 Despite the fact that it is a very useful tool, a recent survey showed that in many ways the Internet is harmful for children.
4 While there have been many important technological developments in the last 50 years, according to a recent study mobile phones are the most important invention.

SPEAKING Answer key p81

⚬⌐ 2

A This presentation is monotonous. She should stress important words and use a lively tone of voice.
B This presentation is the best.
C He is too nervous and hesitant, and disorganized. He should have practised beforehand.

⚬⌐ 3

A Speakers should not turn their backs on the audience.
B Speakers should not read from notes.
C Speakers should face the audience and make eye contact.
D Speakers should not cross their arms.

VOCABULARY DEVELOPMENT Register p82

AIMS
The aim of this section is to improve students' knowledge and understanding of formal and informal registers.

LEAD IN
- Write pairs of words on the board: 'purchase'/'buy', 'deteriorate'/'get worse', 'immediately'/'straightaway'. Ask the students to decide what is similar and what is different in each pair of words.
- Elicit that the meaning is similar but there is a difference in register. Elicit which words are more formal.

PROCEDURE
1 Students read the **STUDY SKILL** and the instructions, and do the task. Elicit the answers. **⊙ 1**
2 Students read the instructions and make the sentences more formal, using a dictionary if necessary. Elicit answers from the class. **⊙ 2**

EXTENSION ACTIVITY
Ask students to look again at the presentation on new technology that they prepared for the Speaking section of this unit. They should focus on the register of vocabulary they used and decide if it was formal or informal. Ask the students if they could make their presentation more formal by changing some words.

VOCABULARY DEVELOPMENT Answer key p82

⊙ 1
1 I intend
2 various
3 present
4 two hundred
5 discuss
6 attempt
7 examining
8 evolved
9 consider
10 approximately
11 However
12 rise
13 remainder

⊙ 2
Possible answers
1 decreased/fallen, beverage
2 consuming, obese/overweight
3 selected/chosen
4 placed, observed
5 absorbed, transform/convert
6 purchase
7 In addition/Moreover, consider

REVIEW p83

AIMS

The aims of this section are to give students further practice in the skills learnt in this unit, and to give them the opportunity to review the work they have done. A further aim is to encourage students to apply what they have learnt to their other academic studies in English.

PROCEDURE

1 🔊 **10.9** Students read the instructions. Play the CD. Check the answers as a class. 🔑 1

2 🔊 **10.9** Students read the instructions and the questions. Play the CD again. They complete the task. Elicit the answers as a class. 🔑 2

3 Students read the instructions and write three questions in pairs. Elicit questions from some students.

4 Students read the instructions and do the discussion task in pairs. Go round and monitor. Stop them after topic 3 if they are not using the phrases and encourage them to do so. Give constructive feedback at the end.

5 Students read the instructions and rewrite the sentences. Check the answers together. 🔑 5

EXTENSION ACTIVITY

Ask the students to list the skills they have learnt and practised in this unit. For example,
– critical listening
– active listening: asking questions
– pronunciation: homophones
– recognizing an opposing view
– delivery of presentations
– formal and informal registers

Put students in groups to discuss how to apply these skills to the work they do in their academic studies.

REVIEW Answer key p83

🔑 1

1 distributed
2 they were lower quality than DVDs
3 watch films online
4 fewer

🔑 2

1 Because of mail rental services (and online streaming).
2 Because mail rental services are too slow, and are slower than online streaming.
3 Faster Internet technologies such as fibre-optic cables.
4 Because it so convenient. It is instant and you can see what you want whenever you like. Also there are different options in terms of pricing.

🔑 5

1 Consumers are eager to **purchase** the newest technological devices available.
2 The researchers **intend** to demonstrate that e-readers are as easy to use as traditional books.
3 I agree with most of your argument. **However,** I'd like to clarify a few points.
4 The company's developers have **examined** new possibilities in telecommunications.
5 Internet retail has **progressed** so quickly that many traditional shops have had difficulties staying up-to-date.

AUDIO SCRIPTS

 1.1

I want to talk to you today about how you can prepare for life at university and how you can become a successful student. It's not always easy to do, but later on I'll give you some tips – some dos and don'ts – to help you be successful. First of all, I want to define success. Success doesn't mean being better than everyone else. Success means being the best you can be, but not everyone can get top marks all of the time. There will be students who get top marks in your group – you may be one yourself – but don't waste time competing with other people. The only person you should compete with is yourself. Try to improve on what you did last time. This requires a very important quality – motivation.

Where does motivation come from? That's up to you to find out. Sometimes it's external – from outside – pressure from parents, your peers, your lecturers, from exams. But the best kind of motivation comes from yourself – from inside. By the end of the course or study programme, don't be one of those students who says, 'I wish I'd worked harder.' Even if you failed you should be able to say to yourself: 'I did the best I could'.

 1.2

Now I'd like to turn to some practical points. Firstly, let's deal with the things that you should do. One of the most important skills is being able to manage your time – time management. Make a study plan – so you know when you have lectures and when you have time to study – to do assignments, read, and research on the Internet. But don't forget to put aside time for relaxation, exercise, and entertainment. These are important too.

Following on from that, another piece of advice is to meet deadlines. If you have an assignment to do for example – plan your time and start working on it as soon as you can so that you meet the deadline. Don't leave everything to the last minute.

The next bit of advice concerns resources. You should organize the resources you need. During your studies you will need to have access to a lot of information. Where are you going to get this information from? What resources do you have? By resources I mean course books, reference books, dictionaries, and so on – as well as libraries and the Internet. Keeping track of your resources will help you be more efficient in your studies.

Another important resource is people. Find out which people are available – your lecturers, tutors, the librarians. Get to know them and find out when they're available to talk to. Don't forget your fellow students. Form a study group! Not everyone likes to work with other people, but working with other students in a study group can be a useful way of sharing information – and it can be motivating too.

The final point is to find out your strengths and weaknesses. What are you good at? What are you not so good at? We can call this self-assessment. If you know that your weaknesses are, for example, taking part in discussions, or completing work on time, then you can take steps to improve that.

Finally I'd like to deal with some of the 'don'ts'. Things that good students should not do …

 1.3

Today I'd like to speak about intelligence. First, I'd like to discuss how intelligence is measured, because, I think that this is a good place to begin to think about how we define the term. I'll begin with a brief history of intelligence testing.

The traditional view of intelligence was based around the IQ test. IQ stands for intelligence quotient. Quotient just means number – a way of measuring intelligence. It was devised in 1912 by the German psychologist William Stern. It was a way of measuring children's intelligence.

Nowadays it's used to measure the performance of both adults and children. The IQ score is a prediction of where the individual is compared to other people. Have a look at this graph. It shows the distribution of IQ amongst the population in general. The horizontal axis – here – shows IQ scores ranging from 40 here on the left – to 160 on the right. The vertical axis shows the percentage of people who have that IQ score – it ranges from 0% to over 2.5%. Now, you can see from this curve that the average IQ is 100 – represented here as the highest part of the curve. So just over 2.5% of the population have an average IQ. There are fewer people with IQs over 110, 120, and so on, and very few with IQs over 140. At the other extreme – here – you can see, similarly, that few people have IQs of less than 80 for example, and very few less than 60. What does the shape of the graph remind you of? Yes that's right – a bell. The shape of the graph is like a bell – and that's the reason it's known as a 'bell curve'.

However, many people think that this view of intelligence is very limited …

 1.4

Now let's move on to multiple intelligences. This theory was developed in 1983 by Howard Gardner, a professor of Education at Harvard University. He said that the traditional idea of intelligence was far too limited. He believes there are at least seven different intelligences. These intelligences describe the potential in children and adults – what people are able to do. If you look at this table you can see that the seven intelligences are listed in this column and here on the right are their main features – what a person is able to do if they score highly in this type of intelligence. I'll go through the intelligences one by one.

Firstly, there is linguistic intelligence. Basically, linguistic intelligence means being able to use words well – in speaking, reading, writing, and so on. Such a person might speak several languages or be a good presenter.

Next, logical-mathematical intelligence. A person with good logical-mathematical intelligence is good with numbers, and they can deal with scientific or legal problems easily. Some people say that traditional intelligence tests, the IQ test for example, mainly focus on just this type of intelligence.

The third type of intelligence is spatial intelligence. The word 'spatial' involves area or space, for example, being able to use maps and plans effectively – maps in navigation – finding out where you are and where you are going, and plans in architecture – plans of buildings, and so on.

Let's move onto the fourth type of intelligence. This is called bodily-kinaesthetic intelligence. 'Kinaesthetic' means movement – so this intelligence refers to movement of the body. People with good bodily-kinaesthetic intelligence are good at sports, or drama, or dancing. Or they might be good at making things with their hands, such as models.

The fifth type is musical intelligence. Such a person may be good at singing, or composing music, or playing a musical instrument.

The last two are interpersonal and *intra*personal intelligences. Let me explain these terms carefully – they sound rather similar. Interpersonal intelligence means 'between people', a person who is good at communicating with others. Someone who is good at understanding other people and dealing with their problems – they may also be good at teaching. Intrapersonal, however, means 'within' a person – refers to a person who understands himself or herself, who is good at self-management, and capable of reflection, thinking about what they're doing about their life, and their goals.

 1.5

Now I'd like to deal with the implications of this theory. If we accept Gardner's theory, that there are in fact seven intelligences and not just one generalized intelligence, what does this mean? What are the implications?

Gardner says that our schools and colleges focus most of their attention on just two types – linguistic intelligence, that's language, and logical-mathematical intelligence. In addition to this, he says, we should focus attention on the other intelligences as well, providing for students who are gifted in other ways – in music, design, therapy, as some examples.

This leads to a further conclusion – that teachers should teach in a variety of ways. Why? Because this would use all of the intelligences. For example, a teacher shouldn't just rely on lectures, worksheets, and textbooks. They should employ other methods of teaching in the lessons such as using music, or acting, taking the students on field trips, and using cooperative or group learning.

 1.6

A = Andrew   S = Sarah

A Hi, Sarah. What are you studying?

S Economics. We have a test tomorrow.

A Oh, good luck!

S I'm going to need it! I always leave revision to the last minute. You remember we had that talk last week about study habits – strengths and weaknesses and so on?

A Yes.

S Well that's one of my main weaknesses, I think – leaving revision right to the end.

A I can't meet deadlines, that's my big problem. I'm always late with assignments. But I am good at giving presentations. I enjoy talking to people – explaining things. That's one of my strengths, I think.

S I like talking too, but not presentations. I prefer discussing with people. I think I perform well in seminar discussions.

A Do you always work here in the library?

S Yeah, I usually sit at the same desk and bring all my books and my laptop. I like to work here in the evenings after lectures – it's quieter then.

A Oh I like the mornings. I get up about 6 and work for a couple of hours before breakfast. I prefer working at home – in my room. I have everything there and I can take breaks when I want – and have a cup of coffee.

S Yeah, I think it's important to take breaks. I usually take one every hour.

A I see you have a lot of notes there, I never take notes. I find it slows me down!

S Oh no, I think taking notes is important. It helps me to concentrate while I'm reading – and then I can use the notes later. In that talk the speaker said time management was important. What about that? Do you plan your week?

A Not really. I don't have a study plan – maybe I should.

S I don't have one either. But I agree they are a good idea.

A Sarah, do you always like to work on your own? I think it's a bit lonely here in the library. I like to work with other people. I belong to a kind of study group, you know.

S A study group? No, I prefer to work alone. I find if I work with other people they always want to chat about other things so I can't concentrate properly!

A Oh I see. In that case I had better go and let you work.

S OK. See you later.

 1.7

P = Peter   S = Stefan   K = Katrina

P I'm not sure these so-called 'intelligences' are in fact intelligences at all. Take musical intelligence as an example. My cousin is very good at the piano, but I would call this a skill not intelligence. What do you think, Stefan?

S Well, Peter, if you say that intelligence is only mathematical intelligence or logical intelligence then very few people can be called intelligent, but in fact …

K Yes, but …

S Could I just finish? In fact, we see people all around us who are good at certain things – like learning languages or reading maps. I would call these types of people intelligent too. Now I'm not so sure about bodily-kinaesthetic intelligence. Here I think we are talking about skills or talent and not intelligence.

K I'd like to make a point here. I disagree about people who make things with their hands or who are good at sports – bodily-kinaesthetic intelligence. I do think this is a kind of intelligence. Take footballers for example.

P I wouldn't say footballers are very intelligent. It seems to me …

K Well, let me explain. I think it does take a lot of intelligence to pass a football at the right angle and the right speed so that another player can receive the ball. And scoring goals too – that takes intelligence – judging the distance and the position of the goalkeeper. This is a type of intelligence. Don't you agree, Peter?

P No Katrina I don't agree at all. I think we can say footballers are very fit and also they are skilled in some ways, but …

 1.8

My name's Maria. I'm a few weeks into my second year of uni. I'm doing a degree in Engineering. I'm really happy with the course. The lecturers are great, which is obviously motivating, and, well, I really love Engineering so I'm finding it all really engaging. I got good marks in all of my modules last year and I think I am a pretty good student. I don't know if I'll end up with a distinction, but I'm pretty sure I'll be near the top of my class.

There is a lot of work to do. I feel like we've just got back and I already had a presentation last week and I've got to hand in a research paper on Friday. But like I said, I don't mind the work. In fact I enjoy it. I'm in the library most evenings and I try to start my assignments well in advance of the deadlines. It's easy to be motivated when you're really interested in the material.

 1.9

This graph shows the number of international students enrolled at this university by year. And as you can see on the graph the number of international students at this University has been increasing since the mid-1990s. The horizontal axis shows the year. The first year on the graph is 1995 and it goes up to 2009 over here. The vertical axis shows the total number of international students enrolled. You can see back in 1995, it was only 129. In 1996, that figure rose to 140. But then if we look over here, in the year 2000, it jumps to over 280. That figure steadily increases – see here 2004, 2006 – until it peaked in 2007. In 2008, there were slightly fewer, possibly due to the onset of the global financial crisis, but we expect these numbers to go up again within the next couple of years.

 2.1

I'll just give a brief summary of a few of the therapies that we're going to discuss today.

One that you might be familiar with is acupuncture. Acupuncture involves inserting needles into specific points in the body and manipulating them. It's used to relieve pain and to treat certain conditions.

And you've probably also heard of herbal medicine, which involves treatments using plants and plant extracts – a sort of natural alternative to conventional pharmaceuticals.

Has anyone heard of hydrotherapy? This is a therapy which uses water to treat illnesses or relieve pain. Water jets, mineral baths, and underwater massage are common examples.

Moving along, I think hypnosis is a very interesting therapy. What happens is a patient is put into an almost sleep-like condition and in this condition they are open to suggestions. As a result, the hypnotherapist can help them modify behaviours relating to health, stress or pain management.

The last therapy we'll discuss is yoga, which some of you might recognize as a type of exercise, but it's actually used as a therapy as well. This involves holding the body in different positions. It's often used to treat high blood pressure, insomnia and digestive problems, among other things.

🔊 2.2

L = Lee   S = Sunil   M = Miriam

M Who's going to begin our discussion? Sunil, how about you?

S Thank you, Miriam. Well, it seems to me that in the lecture, Dr Hall was basically saying that alternative medicine doesn't really exist. He said that alternative medicine was not real medicine as it was unproven – and we should only consider scientific, or evidence-based medicine.

M Yes, he claimed that only conventional medicine was based on proper scientific research.

S He seemed to be saying that as there is no real evidence for so-called alternative medicine, claims made by alternative therapists should be treated with caution. What are your feelings about this? Miriam?

M Generally speaking, I feel that Dr Hall's right – none of the alternative treatments have had proper scientific tests and shouldn't be considered medicine at all. Do you disagree, Lee?

L Well, there is plenty of evidence for alternative medicine. For example, a couple of years ago my aunt was suffering from a serious illness. She went to several conventional doctors and they could do nothing for her.

M I'm sorry to interrupt, Lee, but that is not scientific evidence – it's anecdotal evidence. Dr Hall talked about this.

L What do you mean by anecdotal?

M Well, with respect, this is a personal story about what happened to your aunt. That doesn't count as evidence, not scientific evidence anyway.

L But it's a true story and she was cured. She's fine now and conventional medicine didn't work at all. She tried everything. Finally she tried homeopathic medicine which was recommended to her and within a few weeks she completely recovered. It was remarkable.

M But I don't think that we can say for sure that it was homeopathic medicine that cured your aunt. It could have been some other factor that cured her.

L No. We tried everything as I said. The homeopathic medicine worked.

S Actually, I agree with Lee – to a point. There does seem to be an awful lot of what you call anecdotal evidence that some of these treatments work and if you have enough anecdotal evidence then, well, something must be going on. Look at Chinese medicine, for example.

L That's right. Chinese medicine has been around for a very long time – thousands of years in the case of acupuncture, for example. These treatments must work if they have been used for so long.

M I take your point, Lee. These treatments may seem to work, but is that real evidence? We have to be sure that it is not just chance. That's why proper scientific tests are important to find correlations and to prove that there is a link between cause and effect.

S Well, I think we should keep an open mind – at least until we have the scientific evidence.

L I think we do have the evidence, Sunil. For example, tests on diabetes patients in the US showed a strong correlation between herbal treatment and improvement in their condition.

S It seems to me that all other treatments – conventional medicines – have had proper scientific tests – and they are proven, whereas alternative medicines haven't been properly tested. So I suppose Dr Hall is right when he says we should be careful. But on the other hand that doesn't mean to say that alternative therapies don't work.

M Well, I tend to agree with Dr Hall. We need evidence.

L Miriam, you always agree with Dr Hall!

M No, I don't. I didn't agree last week when he said that my report was not up to standard.

🔊 2.3

B = Bill   M = Mary   D = Don   F = Flavia

B Hello. Welcome to *Scientific Research* – our weekly podcast looking at what's new in the world of science. This week we are looking at the results of an interesting survey on students' academic performance and how it may be related to … the amount of exercise they get. Yes, that's right – exercise! Does this really mean students should be in the gym instead of the library? Mary Thomas investigates …

M I'm in the library at Manchester University in the north of England. There are lots of students sitting at desks – some at computer screens – and some have been here for hours. All in all it would seem that studying is not a very healthy pursuit. Add to that the fact that many students, because they are away from home, live on very poor diets. You could conclude that studying is not an active or healthy pastime. But now new research suggests that it may also have a much wider effect. Let me explain.

🔊 2.4 [including 2.5]

B = Bill   M = Mary   D = Don   F = Flavia

[2.5 starts] M A study carried out by Dr William McCarthy and colleagues at the University of California in Los Angeles came up with some pretty interesting results. They compared the physical fitness and body weight of students with their scores in Maths, reading and language tests. Altogether they tested nearly 2,000 students between the years 2002 and 2003. About half were female and half male. They were all from different ethnic backgrounds.

First they weighed the students and found that almost 32% were overweight. Then they tested their fitness by asking them to walk or run for one mile. They noted the time they took to complete the mile. The boys averaged just under 10 minutes and the girls 11 minutes to complete the course. Amazingly, 65% of the students were below the California state fitness standard. Now when these results were matched with the test results what did they find? Well, they found that the students who were fit had higher test scores than those who were not fit. And it was the same picture for the weight of the students. Those students who had a desirable weight scored higher on the tests than those who were overweight. It seems to show a correlation between fitness and high grades – in other words, exercise is beneficial for academic performance. But a note of caution, researchers say they are not really sure why this is the case. [2.5 ends]

Let's get the views of some university students in Manchester. I'm here now in the sports centre in Manchester University. It's eight o'clock in the morning and as you can see it is already very busy. I'm going to speak to a couple of students who are working out on the cycling machines. Don, can you tell me how often you come to the gym?

D About twice a week – more if I can. It depends on the workload.

M What do you think of this research that says you may get better grades if you exercise? Is it working for you?

D I'm not sure it's working yet in my case!

M OK, well good luck! I have Flavia here now. Where are you from Flavia, and what are you studying?

F I'm from Brazil – São Paulo – and I'm studying Urban Planning.

M And what do you think about exercise – how does it help you?

F Well, I come here almost every day and I work out for about an hour. I really think it helps me. I usually feel very relaxed afterwards and more alert mentally when I go to lectures later in the day.

M And does it help with your grades?

F Well, I think it has done – so far!

M Well, it seems to be working with those students anyhow. Back to you, Bill.

B Thanks, Mary. Well, that's all for this week's podcast. Remember there's more information about this topic on our university website.

2.6

1 Today we've been looking at research into diet and health and I've outlined some of the major studies that have been carried out in recent years in countries like Japan, the USA and in India. I think it is quite clear from the results of these studies that there is a clear link between …

2 What I'd like to do today is to see if there is a correlation between what we eat and our general health. In particular, I want to look at the link between the consumption of meat and diseases such as cancer. I think this is an important area of study because …

3 Next, I would like to look at the results of a study that was carried out in Japan in 2009. More than five thousand people were interviewed about their eating habits. Now as you know, Japan is mainly a fish-eating society. But increasingly the Japanese, especially the young people in Japan …

4 I'll try to leave ten minutes or so for questions at the end of the presentation, but if anything is not clear please feel free to interrupt me at any time …

5 What we need are more large-scale studies of the type I have mentioned. Hopefully, in the future such studies will lead to a greater understanding of diseases such as cancer and help us in our efforts to find effective treatment …

2.7

Hello. My name's Francesco Mancini. I work for the organization, World Health International. Today I'd like to talk about one particular part of health-care and that is alternative or complementary medicine. Perhaps I'd better start by explaining what these terms mean. 'Alternative' is used by people who want to show that their approach to medicine is different from conventional medicine – an example would be acupuncture. 'Complementary' means that approaches such as acupuncture can be used alongside conventional medicine. Now why should we be talking about alternative medicine? One of the main reasons is the growing interest we have seen in this approach to medicine, especially in the western world. The aim of this talk is to answer this question: Should we take alternative therapies seriously? I'll begin with a brief review of the history of alternative therapies and their growth in recent years. Then I'd like to describe a few of these approaches in detail – what they are and what they claim to do. And finally, I'll be examining some of the evidence. By the way, if you have any questions, there will be five minutes or so at the end of the talk for discussion.

2.8

P = Phil   R = Roberta   G = Gemma

P OK, well the question is whether or not a healthy and nutritious diet contributes to academic success. I think this is a complicated issue and I'm not sure where to start with it. What do you think, Roberta?

R Well actually, Phil, I think it's quite obvious that it does. Successful students use a lot of energy when they're researching, studying and preparing presentations. They need to be wide awake and focused to do these things well. We've just read an article from a medical journal, which explained that students should make sure they get enough protein, because protein provides the energy that the brain requires. So I think students need to eat healthy food to provide them with sufficient protein and energy. Hmmm. You look like you disagree, Gemma.

G I think you have a valid point, Roberta, when you say that students need to get enough energy. However, I'm not so sure that the evidence indicates that this energy has to come from a healthy diet. There are many sources of energy available to students, which probably aren't considered 'healthy' by most people. I mean sugary foods and caffeinated drinks can provide energy, but these aren't healthy, are they?

P This is exactly what I meant when I said that this issue is more complex than it appears at first glance. I don't know if we have enough evidence to conclusively say one way or the other.

G I don't know, Phil. I think it's pretty clear that many students are both unhealthy and successful. We've seen a study which shows that students are eating more junk food than they did in the past. We also know that the number of university graduates has increased by five percent in the past two years. I think this shows that a healthy diet is not necessary for academic achievement.

R I'm sorry, Gemma, but I don't think you can draw that conclusion from …

2.9

We know that therapies involving water or baths have existed since ancient times. They were used by the ancient Greeks, Romans, Chinese and probably others. However, modern hydrotherapy can be traced back to the 19th century, when it was reintroduced by a monk, Father Sebastian Kneipp, who lived in Bavaria, in what is now Germany. His idea, that water can be used to cure people, caught on across Europe, and is still a widely-practised treatment today.

So how does it work? Well, one way hydrotherapy works is it uses the body's reaction to hot and cold to stimulate the immune system or produce beneficial relaxing effects that reduce harmful stress and anxiety. Another way that hydrotherapy is used to heal is through baths: steam baths and saunas. Toxins can be drawn out of the body through sweating and other processes.

Hydrotherapy is commonly used as a therapy for back pain. It can also be effective for anxiety, insomnia, and arthritis.

3.1

P = Presenter   M = Martin Holt

P London is undeniably a global metropolis. It's the ninth largest city on the planet and its citizens speak over 300 different languages. It has an economy roughly the size of Sweden's. But how did it become the city that it is today? On this week's podcast, I'll be discussing this question with social historian Martin Holt. Welcome, Martin. So, to start, could you talk about how the city we know today came to be?

M Well, from the time that it was founded in the first century by the Romans, London has always been an important trading city, mostly because of its location on the Thames. And by the late Middle Ages it had grown into a trading capital. The Royal Exchange, where merchants could buy and sell goods, was opened in 1571.

P Well, when you walk through London today, it doesn't look like a mediaeval city.

M There are several reasons for this. You see, in 1666 the Great Fire of London destroyed the mediaeval city. Over 80% of all homes in the city were lost in the fire. However, the fire provided a clean slate upon which the city could be rebuilt. As people from rural areas migrated to London, a new city grew to accommodate them all.

P Sorry, but could you explain why so many people wanted to move to London at this time?

M To find work. The Agricultural Revolution in the 1700s increased the country's production of food enormously – and this made it possible to support large cities. At the same time, the new efficient farming methods and machines required many fewer farmworkers.

P Which meant large numbers of unemployed workers in the countryside?

M Precisely. Many of these people were forced to leave the countryside to find work in cities. London was the centre of commerce and industry for the newly developing British Empire, so there were people coming in from all over the world. By the year 1800, the population of London had grown to just under a million – an enormous city for that time. By the end of that century the population had shot up to over 6.5 million.

P So, you were explaining how this influx of newcomers changed the city?

M The huge changes started to occur back in the 18th century with the construction of roads and bridges. Until 1714, there was still only one bridge across the Thames in London. The growth of basic infrastructure allowed the city to expand. The rich and middle classes built squares for housing development mostly to the west of the old city. The clerks and lower-middle class workers had houses further out in the suburbs. The poor lived in brick terrace slums towards the east of the city. Soon, the centre of the original city was no longer residential – it had become the financial centre.

P So people had to travel further to get to work.

M Exactly. The development of London's public transport system was crucial to its development as a city. First, there were omnibuses drawn by horses – from 1829. However, they were too expensive for the average worker. The poor walked, which meant the streets were often congested with pedestrians. The author, H G Wells, described the crowds in London as 'a great mysterious movement of unaccountable beings'.

P That does sound like London.

M Euston station, the first railway station in London, opened in 1837. People could live further from the centre where they worked. And more workers were needed at this time specifically for projects such as building the railways. This happened again in the 1860s with the construction of the London Underground, the Tube, the first underground system in the world.

P OK. So can you tell us about some of the challenges that this expansion of population in London brought?

M Well, aside from the challenge of getting people from their homes to their jobs, perhaps the most obvious was the poverty. The streets were filled with beggars. Often whole families had to work long hours in factories in dreadful conditions. And of course disease was still an enormous problem in Victorian times. Cholera was endemic due to the unsanitary conditions in the city. There was no sewerage system. People used the river, which had become very polluted. In fact, the summer of 1858 is known as 'The Great Stink'.

P The Great Stink?

M Yes, because the city smelled so awful – so awful in fact that Parliament had to close down. In response to this, an engineer named Joseph Bazalgette was tasked with building a sewerage system for the city. He oversaw the construction of more than 1,100 miles of underground sewerage tunnels. Cholera disappeared from the city very soon after this and Bazalgette received a knighthood for his efforts.

P Interesting! So can I ask you to comment on 'parallels' between London and today's developing cities?

M Well, I think growing cities today face similar challenges. For example …

 3.2

Well, today I'd like to talk about a very interesting urban development project – a new city called Masdar City. It's located in the desert not far from Abu Dhabi in the United Arab Emirates. It's interesting because it is going to be an eco-city – in fact the world's first zero-carbon city. To start, I'll explain the terms eco-city and zero-carbon. Then I'll give you some background to the project. After that I'll describe the city in some detail. Finally, I'll look at the feasibility of the project.

Let's begin with definitions. An eco-city is a city that is ecologically healthy – a city that takes account of the environment and makes as little impact on it as possible. This means that the inputs – of energy, water and food – are a minimum and the waste outputs – heat, air and water pollution are also as low as possible. A zero-carbon city goes further and reduces all emissions to nothing – to zero. So for example, transport in such a city would produce no pollution at all.

Let's turn to Masdar City itself. It's being built in the desert about 40 kilometres from Abu Dhabi, the UAE's capital city. It will eventually have a population of about 50,000 and there will be at least one thousand businesses and a university. The city is being designed by Foster and Partners, the famous British architecture firm. The total cost of the project will be between £10 and £20 billion, so it is not exactly cheap.

 3.3

Now what about energy? We've already seen that eco-cities or zero-carbon cities use renewable energy sources – for example, wind power.

Well, in the UAE – one of the world's largest producers of fossil fuels, but also one of the hottest and driest countries in the world – they have decided to use the sun as a source of renewable energy, which seems an intelligent and far-sighted attitude. They have built the biggest solar farm in the Middle East to power the city. They are also experimenting with different ideas for generating power – for example, using mirrors to concentrate light and thereby producing heat to drive generators.

Next, I'd like to look at the cooling of the city. In the desert, of course, daytime temperatures are very high, more than 45 degrees in the summer, so how can a city of 50,000 people and 1,000 businesses be cooled efficiently?

Interestingly, Masdar City will use a variety of centuries-old strategies to keep the city comfortable. One method is the design of the city itself. Traditional Arab cities are very compact – the buildings are close together providing plenty of shade and helping keep cities cool.

Secondly, the walls will be covered with a special material, a terracotta mesh. This is a building material with holes in it. This material will keep the sun out but let the wind in and so will help keep the temperature down.

A third solution proposed is wind towers. These are traditional Arab buildings – tall, square towers with open sides at the top – they will catch any wind and direct it down into the streets and buildings.

Now let's move to another important area of 21st century life – What about transport? How will the inhabitants of Masdar City move about the city?

Well, firstly, it's very compact so people will be able to walk to most places. Streets will be pedestrianized – traffic-free. There will however be some transport – there will be special 'podcars'. These are driverless vehicles powered by solar energy. They stop and start automatically and are programmed to go where you ask. I rather like the sound of these podcars.

So finally, what about the future? Well, the city is due to be completed around 2020 to 2025. In addition to helping the environment by being carbon-zero – the designers claim it will be a happy and healthy place for the inhabitants to live in. The air will be clean and pollution will be minimal.

 3.4

Well, today I'd like to talk about a very interesting urban development project – a new city called Masdar City.

Let's begin with definitions. An eco-city is a city that is ecologically healthy …

Let's turn to Masdar City itself. It's being built in the desert about 40 kilometres from Abu Dhabi, the UAE's capital city.

Now what about energy? We've already seen that eco-cities or zero-carbon cities use renewable energy sources – for example, wind power.

Next I'd like to look at the cooling of the city. In the desert, of course, daytime temperature are very high, more than 45 degrees in the summer, so how can a city of 50,000 people and one thousand businesses be cooled efficiently?

Interestingly, Masdar City will use a variety of centuries-old strategies to keep the city comfortable. One method is the design of the city itself. Traditional Arab cities are very compact – the buildings are close together providing plenty of shade and helping keep cities cool.

Secondly, the walls will be covered with a special material, a terracotta mesh. This is a building material with holes in it. This material will keep the sun out but let the wind in and so will help to keep the temperature down.

A third solution proposed is wind towers. These are traditional Arab buildings – tall square towers with open sides at the top – they will catch any wind or slight breeze and direct it down into the streets and buildings.

Now let's move to another important area of 21st century life – what about transport? How will the inhabitants of Masdar City move about the city?

So finally, what about the future? Well, the city is due to be completed around 2020 to 2025.

 3.5

C = Carlos   S = Suzi   P = Peter

C What do you think about climate, Suzi?

S Well, Carlos, I think it's quite important but not as important as some of the other factors – for example, transport. It seems to me that all the best cities have good transport systems.

C Transport's not so important for me. Climate and culture and recreation – now these really are important. These should go at the top of the list.

S They are important but as I see it the most important thing is personal safety. You can have a nice climate and a lot of good recreational facilities, but I think if you are worried about your personal safety then you can't enjoy living in a city. I really think we should put personal safety at the top of the list. What do you think, Peter?

P Well, as I see it, all cities are dangerous to some extent, Suzi. You probably have to accept that wherever you live. So I agree with Carlos, I don't think personal safety should be high up the list. Perhaps we should put transport first and then climate second. Right, Carlos?

C Climate is very important. Who wants to live in a cold city where it rains all the year? Now Miami – that's a great place …

3.6

First, I'd like to talk about the climate of Dubai. Dubai can be uncomfortable during the summer months of June, July and August when the temperature rises to over 40 degrees, as you can see from this chart. But from October to April the weather is much cooler and then in the winter months – in December, January and February – the temperatures are very pleasant, below 30° by day and quite cool in the evening. Dubai has a dry climate, but there is some rain. The rainfall occurs mainly in the winter months as this second chart shows. February is the wettest month, but there is only 25mm of rain on average.

Now let's turn to the question of transport. Dubai has got many new roads, buses, and most importantly a new, efficient and air-conditioned metro. All of this means that it's easy to get around Dubai and transport is affordable as well …

3.7

The population of many urban centres has increased dramatically in recent years. In fact, currently, over half of the world's population lives in cities. And another trend is the global increase in car ownership. There are now over 600 million cars in the world, which is almost one car for every ten people. It's when we put these two trends together that we start to see a real problem. Of course I'm referring to the amount of car traffic in cities around the world today. So, beyond the obvious annoyance of having to wait in queues, let's look at some of the other problems related to our overcrowded roads.

Pollution is one of the biggest resulting problems. Toxic fumes from automobiles have a negative impact on our health and on the air quality in our cities. This leads to rising healthcare and city maintenance costs. A study in the United States showed that traffic congestion annually costs the economy up to $1,000 per driver. Part of this is because people's time is wasted when they are stuck in traffic. They are often late for work and their time is not used in a productive way.

So what can be done about the problem of traffic congestion in cities? Well, urban planners have tried a variety of strategies. In London, for example, drivers pay a charge to use the roads in the city centre. A lot of people think this is a rather extreme solution but some cities are looking for an even more advanced approach. Urban planners in places such as Nagoya, in Japan, are trying to redesign the cities so that they can function without the use of any private cars at all.

3.8

Today I'm going to quickly talk about the city of London and some of the improvements which are being made to the city. First of all, I'll discuss transport and how the public transport system is being upgraded. Then I'd like to look at public spaces in London.

So I'd like to begin with transport. As some of you might know, London has the oldest underground system in the world. However, this means that some of the tunnels are small and the trains are very old-fashioned. They lack air conditioning and can frequently break down. But the city plans to improve several aspects of the underground system over the next ten years. Current train carriages will be replaced with more spacious and comfortable ones. Stations will be modernized, as some of these haven't seen upgrades in over 40 years.

Now let's move on to public spaces in London. The city is very fortunate in that it has some of the finest parks in any city in the world. This was a result of the fact that the parks belonged to the monarch – the king or queen – so building on the parks was never allowed. Currently, parks throughout London are seeing improvements, especially in areas such as cycle paths and modern, safer playgrounds for children. A separate project is focusing attention on places of historical significance within parks, and providing information for visitors.

4.1

P = Presenter   S = Sam   M = Mariam   L = Lee

P Hello and welcome to *Global View* – our weekly look at what is happening around the world. Today our topic is the global food crisis. What has caused this crisis – and what solutions can we find? Here with me in the studio is our panel of economists and journalists. First I'd like to introduce Sam Robinson, a journalist with the New York Telegraph.

S Hi.

P And next, Mariam Mangoli, an economist working for an African bank.

M Good evening.

P And finally, Lee Jin, a specialist on food production in the developing world.

L Hello.

P Well, let's start with you, Sam. What are the causes of the present food crisis throughout the world?

S I think there are a number of causes. One is the low productivity of farmers in the poorest countries in the world. It's not their fault really. They can't afford seeds, and fertilizers – and they can't pay for the water they need for irrigation.

P Mariam, what other factors are there?

M I agree with Sam. Low productivity is a problem, especially in Africa. But there are also what I would call natural causes. One is climate change. The recent droughts in Australia and Europe cut the global production of grain and this has contributed to the problem.

P Lee, I'd like to bring you in here. What do you see as the causes of this crisis?

L Another factor is population growth. In your introduction you called it a global food crisis, but there is also a global population crisis which has had an impact on food prices. There are clearly more mouths to feed, and together with rising incomes, there is a greater demand for food globally. Again we could call this a factor, like climate change, that we don't have a lot of control over. But there is one other cause of the crisis, which is clearly due to man's activities, and that is the production of biofuels.

S Can I come in here? I agree with Lee – biofuels have been a disaster. Governments in recent years have encouraged farmers to produce crops for fuel instead of crops for food. This has had a huge impact on food production.

P OK. Well, we seem to agree that there are four main causes of the present food crisis – low productivity, climate change, population growth, and also biofuels. But I'd like to move on now to consider solutions.

🎧 4.2

P = Presenter   S = Sam   M = Mariam   L = Lee

P What can we do? What practical steps can we take to solve this problem – this food crisis? Mariam?

M I'd like to come back to what I said earlier about climate change and drought. One thing we could do is to look at ways of making the world's crops 'weather-proof'. We could take steps to ensure that crops don't suffer during droughts. For example, in Africa – a simple thing like a farm pond. In the wet season the pond would collect water and this would be available in a drought.

P That seems like a very effective and very simple solution. Lee?

L I mentioned earlier the problem with biofuels, so I think another simple solution would be to stop this investment in biofuels. Let famers produce food again – not fuel. It is food that the world needs from them. As far as fuel is concerned, governments have to find alternatives to solve this crisis – but not biofuels.

P OK. But let's go back to the first point we made – about low productivity. Sam – what can we do about this central issue? Are there any easy ways to increase productivity?

S Yes, there are. As I said at the beginning of our discussion, just give the famers seeds, fertilizers and water – that's what they need. Now some people will say that this is a very expensive solution. But in fact it is not as expensive as the alternative for these countries, which is importing food. Let's look at the example of Malawi. Agriculture was very unproductive. Malawi had to import basic food – like maize! So what did the government do? They gave farmers subsidized seeds – high yield seeds – and subsidized fertilizers. Within two years Malawi was exporting maize, not importing it.

P So maybe Malawi is a model for other countries.

🎧 4.3

Hello. My name's Joshua Toure. I'm from the African Agricultural Agency based in Nairobi. As you all know there is a global food crisis caused by a number of factors which have all come together at the same time. But what I want to do today is to show you how we can tackle this crisis by using small-scale projects – small, local initiatives which are supported by international aid agencies. My examples today all come from the southern African state of Malawi.

🎧 4.4

Let me begin by showing you the location of Malawi. It's here in south-eastern Africa. It lies along the shores of Lake Malawi and is bordered by Zambia, Mozambique and Tanzania.

And here on this slide are a few facts and figures about the country. The capital city is Lilongwe – that's L-I-L-O-N-G-W-E. It's a rapidly growing city – the population is now nearly 1 million. Not so long ago it was just a small village on the banks of a river. The population

of the country as a whole is just over 12 million. But it is not a very large country in area – about 118,000 sq km. It's about the same size as Cuba or North Korea. The life expectancy of its population is 36 – yes that's right just 36 years – due mainly to the high incidence of disease in the country.

Now if we look at the climate chart for Malawi we can see that there are two distinct seasons in the year: the rainy season, which lasts from December to May; and the dry season from June to November. In some years when rainfall is lower than average, farmers face great difficulties.

Malawi is an agricultural country. Tobacco is its most valuable export. But its main staple crop, that is, the crop that provides food for its people, is maize – corn. So maize has a very important role in the economy.

🎧 4.5 [including 4.6]

Now what are the problems facing farmers? Here you can see the three main problems: lack of regular water supplies, poor soil quality and thirdly yields – that is the amount of produce farmers get from their land – yields are low.

First, the problem of water. This slide shows a family working in their field. The crop in the field is maize. In the past the family was only able to produce one harvest a year, during the rainy season. But a new irrigation project, using water from a stream to irrigate the fields of eight villages in the region, has transformed their lives. This family are now able to harvest up to three times a year.

And here you can see the channel that was built to bring water to their fields. It has really transformed the lives of this family and other people living in the area! Now they can grow crops in the dry season.

Another way that food production has been increased in Malawi is by the distribution of subsidized high yield seeds and legumes – that's plants like beans, peas, lentils, and so on. The seeds and legumes are sold to farmers at low prices. Similarly, the government distributes subsidized fertilizers.

[4.6 starts] What are the results of these initiatives to help farmers? Quite dramatic, as you can see from the graph. Corn production in Malawi had fallen sharply from a high point in 2000 of around 2.5 million metric tonnes down to around 1.5 million in 2002 and 2003. In 2005, the year this policy was introduced, the total was just 1.7 million metric tonnes, still well below the 2000 level. However, the following year, 2006, production jumped dramatically to 2.7 million metric tonnes, and again in 2007, to 3.4 million metric tonnes. A 27% increase from the previous year – a remarkable achievement.

So, what does all this show? Is Malawi a model for the rest of Africa? I think it is. Small-scale projects are the answer – projects designed to give farmers what they need. And the three things they need most are – first, seeds, that is, high yield seeds – second, fertilizers – and thirdly, of course, a regular supply of water.

To conclude, the global food crisis can be solved if we adopt this slogan – Think Globally–Act Locally. As I said at the beginning it is a global crisis but it needs to be tackled by small projects that take into account the knowledge and the needs of local people and if we can do that then … **[4.6 ends]**

🎧 4.7

Today I want to talk about biofuels. There are two main types – ethanol and biodiesel. Ethanol can be used in ordinary cars. It comes from crops, plants such as sugar cane and grains. Biodiesel on the other hand comes from plants such as oil palm and soybean. The countries which use biofuels the most include Brazil, the USA, and France. Biofuels are generally used for transport – for cars, lorries, buses and planes.

Now what about the process of making biofuels? Take ethanol as an example. Well, firstly the plants are grown like normal crops. When they are ready they are collected – harvested – and then transported to a refinery – a bio-refinery – where the plants are converted by chemical processes into ethanol. This is then distributed to petrol stations and sold as biofuel to motorists …

 4.8

S = Samira   M = Mike   H = Hiroto

S Who would like to start the discussion? Mike?

M Well, it seems to me that the introduction of biofuels has been a mistake. I can see why this was done but these crops take up a lot of valuable agricultural land that could be used for producing food. And what's more because the land is being used for biofuel crops it pushes up food prices. Hiroto, what do you think?

H I agree. Rising food prices are a real problem, especially for the poorer regions of the world. We have seen food riots as people have protested about rising food prices. But in the long term, I can't see any other alternative. We know that oil, gas, and coal will run out one day. We have to explore other sources. Samira, what do you think?

S What about solar power, wind power, and other renewable sources?

H These have a part to play but so far they make up just a small percentage of our needs. I think biofuel is easily produced and probably a lot cheaper than other renewable sources, solar energy for example. Samira?

S Well I agree that biofuels are easily produced. And also they can be grown locally. There is no need to transport the fuel halfway around the world like we have to with oil, for example. So there are a lot of positive points, but on the other hand I do feel they are pushing up the price of food and this is a very important concern. And we have to think about the effect these crops may have on the soil. It's really quite a difficult choice …

 4.9

1 109, 773   **2** 15,675,000   **3** 36%   **4** 78.95   **5** 0.245   **6** ¾

 4.10

Hello. Today I'm going to talk briefly about my country, Tunisia. I'll start off by giving you some facts and figures about the country before going on to talk about agriculture in detail. Now I expect you all know where Tunisia is. It's in North Africa, located between Algeria in the west and Libya in the east. It borders the Mediterranean Sea. The area of the country is not very large, 163,610 sq km. I'll repeat that if you didn't catch it – 163,610 sq km. So it is larger than Greece, for example, but a lot smaller than Libya, our neighbour to the east. The population of the country taken from the 2006 estimate is just over 10 million, 10,175,014 to be exact – that's 10,175,014, but I am sure it has increased since then.

The climate of Tunisia varies from the north to the south. In the north we have mild rainy winters and hot dry summers – so it is a typical Mediterranean climate. The south, however, is a desert region and it is hot and dry all year. Life expectancy is high in Tunisia – 75.12 years. Some people say this is because of our healthy diet. Finally, in this introduction, I'd like to mention the main crops – these are firstly, wheat, then tomatoes, and lastly olives. Last year, wheat production in metric tonnes was 1,360,000, tomatoes – 920,000, and thirdly olives – 700,000 metric tonnes.

Now I'd like to move on to a more detailed description of agriculture in Tunisia …

 4.11

One point one billion people throughout the world don't have sufficient access to safe, clean drinking water. This is referred to as the 'water crisis'. Experts have identified several causes for the water crisis. One cause is deforestation. You see, trees hold water in the ground. When an area of trees is cut down to make room for farms or urban development, this reduces the amount of underground water. This is especially noticeable in tropical rainforests, which produce about 30% of our planet's fresh water. Unfortunately, many tropical rainforests are undergoing serious deforestation. So what

can be done to solve this problem? Well, reforestation has been taking place on a small scale in some regions, but before that, I think education is the real answer. Citizens and governments need to be educated in how deforestation can lead to very serious problems. Only after there is a broad understanding of the risks, can we begin to undo some of the damage which has already been caused.

 5.1

J = Jane   L = Lee   S = Sunil   M = Miriam

J I think we need to discuss two questions. Firstly, to what extent is the globalization of culture actually happening? Lee, how do you see it?

L Well, Jane, personally, I think we have to be careful here not to exaggerate the globalization of culture. I think it is a good thing, but it may not be as widespread as the media seem to think. There are still many areas of the world that have kept their own culture. China, for example. What do the rest of you think? Miriam?

M I think it is happening – the cultural boundaries the author mentions in the article – these boundaries have gone. I see it all around – fashion, for example.

S Yes, all these designer clothes – Adidas, Versace, Jimmy Choo – you see them everywhere.

M And it is the same with entertainment. I read recently that *House* is the most popular TV programme in the world – it is watched in more than 60 countries – 60!

J What about food? I think there are certain foods that are popular all over the world. I think that is a sign of globalization too. What do you think, Sunil?

S Certainly. Take pizza for example – pizza was once only an Italian snack – and now you find it in almost every country you go to. I read recently that Pizza Hut has 34,000 restaurants in 100 different countries. And I think the result of that can be the suppression of local culture. Lee, what's your view on this?

L Well, as I said earlier, I think there is some globalization of culture, but I think local culture is still strong. I visited Moscow recently – and yes, it's true that there are McDonalds and Pizza Hut and so on – but at home people eat Russian food. That hasn't changed. Miriam?

M Well, Jane, I think most of us seem to be in agreement on this question. There is a trend towards the globalization of culture.

J So, what about the second question – is this move towards a global culture (if it is happening) a good thing? Or does it mean that local cultures will disappear? Would anyone like to comment?

M Well, to me it seems we all end up the same – doing the same thing and eating the same food. On the whole, I am against this trend. Sunil?

S Well, I look at it this way – globalization of culture brings people together – you will have a shared culture. This means that wherever you go in the world you will feel at home. There will be people who speak English, you will recognize the restaurants and coffee shops, you can use the Internet and your mobile phone. And when you meet people in these countries you will have things in common – things to talk about – the World Cup, for example, or cricket, or the Olympics.

L Yes. And you can see the same films and satellite TV programmes – and also buy the clothes you like to buy in your home country. My brother is in China and he saw the film *Avatar* there. He saw it before I did!

M I think we are getting away from the issue here. If I go to another country I like to see something new – a different culture – different food, different things to buy in the shops – a different way of life. I don't want everything I can get at home!

J So what you are saying is that globalization makes travel less interesting.

M Exactly. We are all going to be the same so there will be nothing new to learn.

J I think I agree with Miriam on this. The world will become less interesting. Sunil, what's your view on this?

S Well, I'm afraid I don't agree. There will still be a lot to learn – and you will have a choice. If you want to try local food, you can – but if you are in a hurry or you are not adventurous you can have the food you know.

M And another thing – what about language? That's part of culture too. If everybody speaks English, local languages will suffer. Some may disappear.

L That's true. A lot of smaller languages are already disappearing.

M And local customs and local values – all of that will go – replaced by Western values.

S No, that's not true, Miriam. We will still have our local values – the things we learn from our parents – but in addition we will have common international or global values. I think that's great. After all, we are all living on the same planet!

J Well, I agree with Sunil we are all living on the same planet and things that bring us closer together are good. On the other hand I think Miriam has a point. It is a pity to see local culture destroyed.

L No! Local cultures are not destroyed. They are – what's the word in the article? – supplemented by another culture – an additional culture – which is global culture.

J We seem to be divided on this. Let me just summarize what we've been saying in this discussion. I think we all agree that globalization of culture is happening to some extent – but not all of us think it is a good thing. Those in favour say that it is a good thing because it means that we will have …

🎧 5.2

J = Jane   L = Lee   S = Sunil   M = Miriam

J So, what about the second question – is this move towards a global culture (if it is happening) a good thing? Or does it mean that local cultures will disappear? Would anyone like to comment?

M Well, to me it seems we all end up the same – doing the same thing and eating the same food. On the whole, I am against this trend. Sunil?

S Well, I look at it this way – globalization of culture brings people together – you will have a shared culture. This means that wherever you go in the world you will feel at home. There will be people who speak English, you will recognize the restaurants and coffee shops, you can use the Internet and your mobile phone. And when you meet people in these countries you will have things in common – things to talk about – the World Cup, for example, or cricket or the Olympics.

L Yes. And you can see the same films and satellite TV programmes – and also buy the clothes you like to buy in your home country. My brother is in China and he saw the film *Avatar* there. He saw it before I did!

M I think we are getting away from the issue here. If I go to another country I like to see something new – a different culture – different food, different things to buy in the shops – a different way of life. I don't want everything I can get at home!

J So what you are saying is that globalization makes travel less interesting.

M Exactly. We are all going to be the same so there will be nothing new to learn.

J I think I agree with Miriam on this. The world will become less interesting. Sunil, what's your view on this?

S Well, I'm afraid I don't agree. There will still be a lot to learn – and you will have a choice. If you want to try local food, you can – but if you are in a hurry or you are not adventurous you can have the food you know.

🎧 5.3

J = Jane   L = Lee   S = Sunil   M = Miriam

S Yes, – all these designer labels clothes – Adidas, Versace, Jimmy Choo – you see them everywhere.

M And it is the same with entertainment. I read recently that *House* is the most popular TV programme in the world – it is watched in more than 60 countries – 60!

S I read recently that Pizza Hut has 34,000 restaurants in 100 different countries.

L Well, as I said earlier. I think there is some globalization of culture, but I think local culture is still strong. I visited Moscow recently – and yes it's true that there are McDonalds and Pizza Hut and so on – but at home people eat Russian food. That hasn't changed.

J Yes. And you can see the same films and satellite TV programmes – and also buy the clothes you like to buy in your home country. My brother is in China and he saw the film *Avatar* there. He saw it before I did!

🎧 5.4 [including 5.5, 5.6, 5.7]

[5.5 starts] We've been discussing globalization recently and the cultural aspects of this phenomenon – the fact that as globalization develops all parts of the world seem to be getting closer and closer to one another culturally. Perhaps you remember the term I used last time – Global Village.

Well, today I want to talk about one example of global culture – and in particular one internationally famous company – Starbucks. I'll start off with a brief history of Starbucks – a timeline from its origins in 1971 – and then I'll look at the current situation – the extent of the Starbucks chain across the world – and finally, I'll discuss the implications of this expansion. [5.5 ends]

[5.6 starts] Starbucks was founded in 1971 by three friends in Seattle in the US. At first, they just sold coffee beans and coffee-making equipment. In 1982, a business entrepreneur Howard Schultz – that's Howard – H-O-W-A-R-D – Schultz – S-C-H-U-L-T-Z – joined the company as Marketing Director. Schultz went to Italy and while there he was very impressed with Italian coffee bars. He came back and tried to persuade the company to open coffee bars, serving Italian-style coffee. His idea wasn't accepted so he left the company and in 1986 started his own chain of coffee bars, which became very successful. The following year – 1987 – Schultz bought the Starbucks chain. Expansion continued and Starbucks started to open coffee bars outside Seattle – in fact, all across North America. 1996 was another important date in the history of Starbucks. This was when the first Starbucks was opened outside North America. It was in Tokyo, Japan. And in 1998 they entered the UK market – buying up a chain of UK-owned coffee shops. From there Starbucks expanded rapidly across the globe. By 2003, they had more than 6,400 outlets worldwide. Between 2001 and 2004, they opened 1,200 new stores every year – that's 1,200 new stores every year. Imagine that! [5.6 ends]

[5.7 starts] So what is the situation today? Has this expansion continued? Well, currently there are over 16,000 Starbucks in more than 50 countries worldwide from Argentina, to the UAE, to China. 50 countries! So it really is a global brand. Starbucks have plans for as many as 30,000 stores across the world – 30,000, with China becoming second only to the US in the number of outlets.

Nowadays, Starbucks is not just a coffee shop. They serve coffee of course, but they also serve snacks and soft drinks. They offer free WiFi access in their stores, so coffee drinkers can browse the Internet on their laptops while enjoying a cappuccino.

What kind of company is Starbucks? Starbucks prides itself on being a responsible business. For example, the coffee they buy is Fair Trade certified and all the cups they use are either recycled or reusable.

Finally, in this brief overview of Starbucks, I'd like to look at the implications of the rise of Starbucks and similar companies.

What does it all mean? Well, Starbucks is an example of a truly global company. Let me quote from their website: *'Our stores are a welcoming place for meeting friends and family, enjoying a quiet moment alone with a book, or simply finding a familiar place in a new city.'* That last point is important. Starbucks offers customers *'a familiar place in a new city'*.

Opponents of globalization say that companies like Starbucks are bad for local businesses. They argue local coffee shops will go out of business because they cannot compete with a global giant. They also claim that they are limiting choice – all coffee shops will eventually become the same. On the other hand there are those who say that companies like Starbucks are simply giving people what they want – comfortable coffee shops where they can meet friends, enjoy coffee and use their laptops. Because it's a global brand, they know wherever they are in the world they can get the same product and the same standard of service.

In conclusion, we have to say – even if some people don't like the idea of a global culture as represented by companies like Starbucks, it's a fact of life. The world really is becoming a global village. [5.7 ends]

 5.8

A = Andy   B = Beth

A Hello. I'm from Manchester University. We're conducting a survey on street markets. Could I ask you a few questions?

B Yes, certainly.

A Thank you. First of all, do you live in Manchester?

B Yes, I do. I live in Didsbury.

A Now, how often do you shop in this market – daily, three or four times a week, once a week, monthly, or less often.

B Less often – probably about once a month.

A Right. And why do you like shopping here?

B Well, the products are nice and fresh – and the prices are good too. They're often cheaper than in the supermarkets.

A OK. Now how important is price for you when you are shopping? Can you say on a scale of 5 to 1 – where 5 is very important.

B Hmmm – you say 5 is very important? Well, in that case 4.

A Now, how do you get to the market? Walking, by bus, by car or other.

B I have to get a bus here. It takes about 20 minutes.

A I see. And can I ask about the type of products you buy? What do you usually buy here?

B Well, I like the fish. I think it's fresh. And I buy fruit as well. And there's a nice stall where they sell bread. I usually buy some bread.

 5.9

Now let's turn to the results of the survey. You can see from this pie chart that almost all of the shoppers we spoke to – our survey sample – came from Manchester – nearly 90%. Only a few came from outside the city.

The second chart shows how often the shoppers came to the market. You can see that the majority of our sample shop in the market on a weekly basis – around 55%. Surprisingly, quite a few shop there on a daily basis – just about 20%. And 15% come three or four times a week. The others came monthly or less often.

Next, we asked the shoppers how important price was for them on a scale of 5 – very important – down to 1. As you can see from the bar chart most people chose 5 or 4 – about 50% said 5 – very important – and 35% said 4 – important. Just 15% chose 3 and interestingly no one chose 2 or 1.

Then we wanted to find out how people came to the market. We gathered this data on Wednesday and on Saturday to see if there is any difference. The table shows quite clearly that the majority of shoppers, just over 55%, walked to the market on Wednesday. We think this might be because they work in the area. On Saturday, that figure was lower, around 35%, as people were less likely to walk to

the market from their homes. About 30% said they came by bus on a weekday, while at the weekend it was noticeably higher. Only a few came by car – about 10% on both days. The rest of the people came by other means of transport – by bicycle or taxi.

We asked people why they liked shopping in the market. We had a number of different answers but the main points that came up were that the produce was cheap and also fresh …

 5.10

M = May   A = Alberto   R = Rita

M So, we've discussed how technology has lead to the globalization of culture, but could there be other factors as well? What do you think, Alberto?

A Well, I don't know, May. I think technology obviously has a role in it, but so do migration and travel. People are moving around a lot more than they used to. The reason there are Vietnamese restaurants in London is because people from Vietnam moved to London, not because people living in London read about Vietnamese food on the Internet …

M Well …

A Would you like to comment on that, May?

M Yes, thanks. I see what you're saying, but it's a matter of scale. The huge increase in globalized culture is very recent. Populations have been moving around for ages, but only in the last – what, thirty years? twenty years? – have we seen this kind of uniform culture across the globe. As a result of this, I think technology has to be considered the most important cause. Rita, what's your view?

R You both make good points, but I don't think we should leave out market factors.

A I'm not sure if I'm following you, Rita. Could you explain that?

R Globalized culture has been spread by big companies looking for new markets to sell their products into. Look at Starbucks. They are a big international company who want to find new places to sell their coffee. Every time they open a branch in a new place, the globalization of culture spreads that much further.

 5.11

Another international company that I imagine you've heard of, or been to, is the Swedish furniture company, IKEA. So IKEA was started by Ingvar Kamprad – that's I-N-G-V-A-R – K-A-M-P-R-A-D. It was founded in 1943 and the first IKEA store was opened in Almhult. I'll spell that too, it's A-L-M-H-U-L-T, in Sweden, in the year 1958. By 1963, there was an IKEA store in Norway. It spread rapidly throughout the 1970s and 80s and now – you'll want to note this down – there are over 250 stores in over 40 countries.

6.1 [including 6.2, 6.3]

P = Presenter   T = Tomas Olearski

[6.2 starts] **P** Hello and welcome to World Report. With me in the studio today is Dr Tomas Olearski – an architect and historian who has worked closely with World Heritage for many years. Tomas, let me start by asking you about World Heritage. What exactly is it? And when did it begin?

T Well, the initial idea for the World Heritage Programme came about in 1954. The Egyptian government were planning the construction of the Aswan High Dam on the River Nile. This project, which would help to control the seasonal flooding of the river and generate electricity, unfortunately endangered the Abu Simbel and Philae Temple complexes.

P So these temples would have been flooded by the reservoir created by this dam?

T That's right. They would have been lost forever. This came to the attention of the United Nations, and it was decided that the temples had to be saved. The rationale was that these monuments were humanity's heritage, rather than one nation's, and we all share responsibility to protect our common heritage.

P So, what happened to the temples?

T They were physically moved to a new site – higher land – away from the dam. More than $80 million was provided by countries contributing to the United Nations. These temples are unique – to let them be covered by flood-water would have been a great loss for all of mankind. The World Heritage Programme grew out of the success of this project and finally in 1972 the convention – the World Heritage Convention – was ratified. That is to say, the nations in the UN agreed on a text outlining the goals of the programme.

P Could you briefly explain what some of these goals are?

T The basic goal of the UNESCO World Heritage Programme is to help preserve heritage sites – to keep them for future generations. This goal is achieved by a number of steps. First the organization provides money and resources to maintain sites which are in immediate danger – sites such as Abu Simbel. It also helps with the day-to-day maintenance of heritage sites by providing technical assistance and training programmes. And thirdly, it helps to raise public awareness of these sites. The publicity generated for sites on the World Heritage list can result in a substantial increase in tourist revenues.

P It sounds as though it is very beneficial for countries participating in this programme. About how many countries are part of this scheme?

T The number has increased over the years. To date, 187 have ratified the convention.

P So 187 have agreed to the aims of the convention?

T That's right. **[6.2 ends]**

[6.3 starts] P Now, can you tell me why, in your opinion, we need an international organization for this? Can't countries look after their own heritage – their own important sites?

T A good question. But the fact is that many countries – for whatever reason – do not, or cannot, protect their cultural or natural sites. There may be wars in that region, or maybe the government does not consider it an important issue, or more likely they simply do not have the resources to protect these sites. Also we believe that these wonderful places – the mountain railways of India, or the Jurassic coast of Dorset in the UK, for example, belong to all of us – are a part of the world's heritage. It is our duty to protect these places for future generations.

P Now, I believe there are about 900 World Heritage sites all over the world …

T Yes. 911 at the moment. The number is increasing all the time.

P And how many of these 911 are cultural sites?

T There are 704 cultural sites and 180 natural sites. And there are also 27 sites which we say are 'mixed'. They are of both cultural and natural importance.

P Where are these heritage sites? Are they mainly in Europe and America?

T No, no. They are all over the world – Asia, Africa, South America – in 151 different states to be exact. Let me explain what these sites are. The cultural sites may include buildings such as the Sydney Opera House – or monuments such as the Abu Simbel Temples, or perhaps whole cities – like Verona in Italy. Cultural sites also include places which have special significance for mankind – for example the Hiroshima Peace Memorial in Japan. The natural sites, on the other hand, include forests, mountains, lakes, deserts and so on. So for example, the tropical rainforest of Sumatra in Indonesia is a World Heritage Site, Mount Kenya in Africa, and Lake Baikal in Russia. An example of a mixed site would be Cappadocia in Turkey where there are unique features of geology and also unique settlements – houses built into rocks.

P How do you select these sites? How do you decide that this building or forest or desert is important, but another place is not?

T It is difficult. But we use ten criteria altogether. For example, a cultural site could show an important stage of human history – the development of early man, for example – or a natural site

might be important for conserving a threatened species – the tiger for example. This is an important criterion.

P What is the procedure for getting a site recognized as a World Heritage Site? For example, if I think a certain building in my city should be on the list, what should I do?

T I'm afraid nomination starts with countries not individuals. So first a country should make a list of important cultural and historical sites which it thinks should be a World Heritage Site. We call this a Tentative List – a list of possible sites. Well, from that list of possibles the country then selects one site that it thinks is really important and adds it to a Nomination File. The file is inspected and the nominations are passed to the World Heritage Committee. The committee meets once a year and decides whether to add this site to the list of World Heritage Sites or not. **[6.3 ends]**

 6.4

I'm very pleased to welcome our speaker today, Rosie Sanders. Professor Sanders is a well-known archaeologist from the University of London. She's a specialist in the Middle East and has visited the region on many occasions. Today's illustrated talk is part of the series 'Saving the Past'. It is about Bahla Fort, which is located in the interior of Oman. This fort is now a UNESCO World Heritage Site. In this talk, Professor Sanders will describe the town of Bahla and then look at the history of the fort. Finally, she will describe the continuing restoration of the fort with the help of UNESCO and the Omani government.

 6.5

Hello. Thank you for that kind welcome. Today I want to talk to you about a very interesting fort located in Oman. The name of the fort is Bahla and it is now a UNESCO World Heritage Site.

The oasis town of Bahla, set in the heart of Oman, is famous for many reasons. As you can see from this picture, Bahla is surrounded by date palm trees. The water in this dry, arid part of Oman comes from the nearby Jebel Akhdar or Green Mountain, which you can see in the distance, and for many centuries this has given life to Bahla. In the past, wheat, barley, cotton, and sugar cane were cultivated here, but today the main agricultural crop is dates.

The next picture shows you the view from the top of the fort. From here you can see how green the whole oasis is. In fact Bahla is really a collection of villages – some 46 villages set within the oasis – and surrounded by a long defensive wall.

This is the souk – the local market – which is really the centre of the town. Here the products from the farms are sold – vegetables, fruit, and of course, dates. There is also a livestock market – for goats, chickens, and so on. And here you can buy the famous Bahla pottery produced by Bahla's own potters.

But more important than the market or pottery is the fort. This picture shows a view of Bahla Fort taken from the souk area. Oman has a lot of forts spread all over the country but this is the oldest and largest fort in Oman.

The fort dates from around the 13th or 14th centuries when Bahla was an important trading centre and the home of the powerful Banu Nebhan tribe. It was very large – the walls are 12 kilometres in length – and the towers are more than 50 metres high. It was built of brick and sandstone – sandstone for the foundations and bricks made of mud for the walls. But over the years because of wars between tribes – and the effects of the sun and rain – the fort walls and towers deteriorated. By the 1980s the whole structure was in very poor condition – in fact a ruin. The towers had collapsed and the walls of the main buildings had fallen down too.

However, in 1987 Bahla fort became a UNESCO World Heritage Site and in 1988 was added to the list of World Heritage Sites in Danger, a list buildings or environments in immediate danger of being lost to the world. So the situation in Bahla was serious. But from this point on things began to improve for Bahla Fort.

In the 1990s work began on restoring the fort. Over $9 million was spent by the Omani government and for many years the structure was covered in scaffolding, as this slide shows. The building was closed to tourists while the reconstruction work was carried out. Eventually in 2004, the fort was removed from the World Heritage list of endangered buildings. The walls, the towers, and the fort itself have all been restored to what they used to be – using original building materials – mud and stone. Some parts had to be completely rebuilt. The reconstruction is nearly finished and the fort really does look as good as new.

Now Bahla Fort will soon be open again to visitors and I'm sure it will become a very popular tourist attraction. The fact that it is a World Heritage Site – one of only four in Oman – has given it a lot of publicity and its future should be secured.

So to summarize, I've told you a little about the oasis town of Bahla and its history, the story of its fort, and how it became a World Heritage Site and was eventually restored. In conclusion, I'd like to say that Bahla Fort represents a great example of what can be done, with effort and money, to preserve our heritage. These treasures from the past must be preserved for future generations to enjoy.

🔊 6.6

A We can see from this chart that Africa has 33 natural sites, 42 cultural sites, 3 mixed sites making a total of 78 sites. The Arab States, on the other hand, have 4 natural sites, 60 cultural sites and only 1 mixed site. The total number of sites is 65. Next we have the Asia-Pacific region. Here there are 48 natural sites, 129 cultural sites and 9 mixed sites, which makes a total of 186 sites. Now let's look at the Latin American and Caribbean region. The number of natural sites is 35. There are 83 cultural sites and 3 mixed sites. The total is 121. Finally, the totals for all of the regions. The total number of natural sites is …

B To begin with I'd like to explain how many sites there are and where they are located. This table shows World Heritage Sites by region and it also shows which are natural sites, which are cultural, and which are mixed – meaning they have both cultural and natural importance. As you can see there are 5 different regions: Africa, the Arab States, Asia-Pacific, Europe and the United States – as one region, and finally Latin America and the Caribbean. The total number of sites is shown here – 890. The majority – 689 – are cultural sites – and only a few are mixed sites. The region with the largest number of sites is Europe, United States and Canada – 440 – followed by Asia-Pacific with 186 sites. The region with the smallest number of sites is the Arab States – only 65. It is interesting to note here that only 4 of the sites in this region are of natural importance. Perhaps this is because in these dry, arid countries there is little flora or fauna to protect …

🔊 6.7

Speaker A Well, that's it really about the Everglades – it really is an interesting place. By the way, if you are in Florida you should go to Key West. It's not far from the Everglades – it's an island, but you can get there by road. There's a bridge that links all the islands until you get there. OK. Thanks for listening.

Speaker B I hope I have given you a clear picture of the problems faced by the Everglades. I described the location of the Everglades and how the region was formed. I also mentioned the wildlife that you can find there. Finally, I discussed the criteria that were used to select the Everglades as a World Heritage Site and why it has recently been placed on the 'in danger' list.

Speaker C To sum up, I've tried to show you that the Everglades is a unique natural environment. I mentioned the history of the region and how the marshes were formed. We also discussed the wide variety of flora and fauna to be found in the region. Lastly

I looked at the status of the Everglades as a World Heritage Site and how it has recently become classified as being 'in danger'. We need to wake up to what we are doing to the Everglades. If we don't act now we may lose this wonderful natural wilderness, and it will be lost forever. Thank you. Are there any questions?

🔊 6.8

M = Martin   A = Andrea Evans

M On the *Your Community* podcast today we're talking to Andrea Evans, who is a member of the town's Preservation Committee.

A Hello, it's nice to be here, Martin.

M Could you explain what it is exactly that the Preservation Committee does?

A It's a five-person committee and we work hard to raise awareness about buildings of historical significance in our town. We also award funding to buildings or groups that want to take part in civic conservation. If the owner of an historic building needs financial help to preserve that building, they can apply to the committee for a grant.

M How much would a typical grant be?

A Well, anywhere up to £50,000 or so.

M And could you tell us the process you use to award this funding?

A The building owner submits a proposal, which includes why the building is historically significant – it has to satisfy certain criteria, you see – if it is an important example of an architectural style, or alternatively, if something significant happened in this place.

M Could you give us an example?

A For example, if an historically significant person lived there. So, if they satisfy some of the criteria, and show that they have a good plan in place for the future, we can begin to discuss how much is needed. But I should point out that we help in other ways as well. We provide educational support.

M What do you mean by that? Do you go into schools?

A No. That's a good idea, though. What I meant is that we provide information and resources to building owners and conservation groups – not only about maintenance and that sort of thing, but basic legal advice and strategic planning for the future. We help them inform the public about their particular site.

M And do you think that there is much public awareness of the historical buildings in our town?

A Well, no I don't actually, but that's starting to change.

🔊 7.1

An airport consists of at least one surface such as a runway for a plane to take off and land, and often includes buildings such as control towers, hangars and terminal buildings. An airport terminal is a building where passengers transfer between ground transportation and the facilities that allow them to board and disembark from aircraft. Within the terminal, passengers purchase tickets, transfer their luggage, and go through security. Terminals provide access to the aeroplanes via departure and arrival gates. Larger terminals have a range of facilities for passengers including restaurants, shops, and relaxation areas.

🔊 7.2

K = Kate   B = Bill

K In today's podcast we'll be looking at three of the largest and most famous airports in the world – in China, Spain and Singapore. In fact, one of them was recently voted the world's best airport. All three are stunning examples of modern airport design by some of the world's leading architectural firms. And we'll be looking at some of the design issues. How can you make sure that tens of thousands of people arrive and leave the airport efficiently? How can you make airport buildings that are sustainable – that use as little energy as possible? And equally importantly, how can you make sure that passengers have a comfortable and attractive environment to relax in before they depart?

Let's start with the first of the three. Here is Bill Thomas to tell us about a stunning new airport.

B This is Beijing Capital International Airport, currently the biggest airport in the world. It was finished in 2008, just in time for the 2008 Olympics. Designed by Foster and Partners, it has turned out to be a very efficient building in terms of operational efficiency and passenger comfort. It is also very sustainable in its design – for example, great use is made of natural light. The design of the airport reflects Chinese culture. From the air it looks like a flying dragon and inside the airport, the use of traditional Chinese colours – red and golden yellow – and the red columns stretching into the distance make you think of a Chinese temple. According to Norman Foster, the architect, this is a building born of its context. It will be a true gateway to the nation. The newly built Terminal 3 building and the Ground Transportation Centre together enclose a floor area of approximately 1.3 million square metres, mostly under one roof – the first building, by the way, to go over the 1 million square metre mark. Passenger numbers at the airport are currently around 42 million passengers per annum so it is also one of the world's busiest.

K Now let's move from Asia to Europe and to Barajas Airport in Madrid, Bill.

B Barajas Airport is the main international airport serving Madrid in Spain. The country's largest and busiest airport is the world's 11th busiest airport with around 29 million passengers a year. The airport name derives from the adjacent district of Barajas, which has its own metro station on the same rail line serving the airport. The main part of the airport, Terminal 4, was designed by Richard Rogers, and it was inaugurated on February 5, 2006. Rogers is a world famous architect known for the use of steel and glass in his buildings. Terminal 4 in Barajas is one of the world's largest airport terminals in terms of area, at 760,000 square metres. The building is meant to give passengers a stress-free start to their journey. This is managed through careful use of illumination, available by using glass panes instead of walls and numerous domes in the roof, which allow natural light to pass through. The roof consists of a series of waves formed by huge wings of prefabricated steel. Internally, the roof is covered in bamboo strips, giving it a smooth and seamless appearance. In contrast, structural trees are painted to create a kilometre-long vista of graduated colour – a fabulous and colourful effect.

K Finally, let's go back to Asia and look at another modern airport which has recently been voted the best airport in the world.

B Changi Airport in Singapore was named the best airport in the world according to a recent survey. The airport's new Terminal 3 finally commenced operations in January 2008 after years of anticipation and a cost of $1.75 billion. It was designed by the architectural and engineering firm, CPG Consultants. Terminal 3's most outstanding feature is a unique 'butterfly' roof which allows soft natural light into the building while keeping the tropical heat out. The one-of-its-kind roof design has 919 skylights with specially-designed reflector panels which adjust automatically to allow an optimal amount of soft and uniform daylight into the terminal building. Another key highlight of Terminal 3 is a five-storey high vertical garden called 'The Green Wall'. Spanning 300 metres across the main building, it can be admired from the departure and arrival halls, and baggage carousels. The Green Wall is covered with climbing plants and is interspersed with four cascading waterfalls.

The area of the building is 430,000 square metres. Terminal 3 adds a capacity of 22 million passengers per annum to Changi Airport, bringing the airport's total annual capacity to about 70 million passengers.

 7.3

1 This is Beijing Capital International Airport, currently the biggest airport in the world.

2 It was finished in 2008 just in time for the 2008 Olympics. Designed by Foster and Partners, it turned out to be a very efficient building in terms of operational efficiency and passenger comfort.

3 The design of the airport reflects Chinese culture. From the air it looks like a flying dragon and inside the airport the use of traditional Chinese colours – red and golden yellow – and the red columns stretching into the distance make you think of a Chinese temple.

 7.4

Today I want to talk about green architecture and specifically about green skyscrapers. We'll be looking at two buildings in particular which are regarded as fine examples of green buildings. One is in China – the Pearl River Tower and the second is the Bank of America building in New York – two of the best examples of green buildings in the world. I'll be describing the buildings and then looking at their special 'green' features. But before that I want to look at the concept of green architecture in general. What are the features of green buildings that make them different from conventional buildings? These are features such as sustainable energy, waste management, building materials and so on. Before I come to that, let's start with a couple of definitions. What exactly do we mean by a green building?

 7.5

A green building can be defined as: 'one which uses less water, optimizes energy efficiency, uses sustainable building materials, generates less waste, and provides healthier spaces for occupants as compared to a conventional building.'

I'll go through each of those points briefly. Firstly, water use – a green building aims to reduce water demand. This can be done by using rainwater, for example, having a facility on the building to collect it. And secondly, by recycling waste water. Waste water from the building is collected, purified, and then recycled within the building. Now energy efficiency – perhaps the most important goal of a green architect. Energy efficiency means cutting down on the energy used by the occupants of the building. This can be done in a number of ways. One is to make use of alternative sources of energy – such as solar power, wind turbines. Another is to reduce the amount of energy used. For example, using natural light where possible, or materials which insulate the building, that is to say, stop heat leaving the building. Thirdly, let's look at sustainable building materials. Now this term 'sustainable' is an important one. Sustainable means being able to continue using something without it having a negative effect on the environment.

So sustainable building materials can either be natural materials like stone, wood, and paper-based products – or they can be recycled materials – building materials which were used before in construction. Finally, waste management. The aim of green design is to reduce the building's waste to a minimum. So for example, water from the building can be used to water the gardens. Other waste can be composted or recycled.

 7.6

Now let's turn to our examples of a green building – the Pearl River Tower in the city of Guangzhou – that's G-U-A-N-G-Z-H-O-U – in China. It's an elegant building as you can see – a 71-storey skyscraper – over 300 metres high – 309 metres to be exact. It is one of the most environmentally-friendly buildings in the world. So what makes it so environmentally-friendly or green? Well, it's partially powered by wind turbines. It also has a number of features that reduce energy use, for example, solar panels and radiant cooling. Radiant cooling is an energy-efficient way of cooling a building by using water running in pipes built into metal ceiling panels.

Let's have a look at another green building – the Bank of America Tower. It is 55 storeys high and it has a height of 366 metres. That's if we include the spire, which is nearly 78 metres in height. The building is located in New York, in the heart of Manhattan. It was completed in 2010.

It is estimated that the tower will use 50% less electricity than a conventional building. Most of the lighting is natural light – the walls are all made of glass. There will also be a generator in the building which will account for 70% of the building's needs. The emissions from this generator – a gas-powered generator – will be cleaner than those from conventional sources. The building will use rainwater and grey water. Grey water, by the way, is the name given to recycled water from wash-basins. This can be used to flush toilets.

7.7

Well, in my view, skyscrapers are essential for modern cities for a number of reasons. The first is population density. A city with a lot of high-rise buildings has a higher density than cities with low-rise buildings. This means that less land is used and there is less traffic as people live closer to work, shops, etc. and don't need cars to get around. Let's look at Hong Kong and Mumbai as examples. Hong Kong, first of all, it has a population of 7 million but only 23% of its land is used for buildings. This means that the urban density in Hong Kong is very high, 70,000 people per square mile, but because of that the rest of the area is preserved as natural landscape for the people to enjoy. Mumbai on the other hand has a lower population density – 6,000 people per square mile, as it has a lot of low-rise buildings. As a result, Mumbai covers a huge area and getting around the city is extremely difficult. Another reason I support skyscrapers is …

7.8

A = Antonio   J = James   C = Carmen

A Well, it seems to me that introducing the Internet in schools is not a good idea. For one thing, children will waste a lot of time playing computer games and chatting to friends online. What do you think, James?

J I see your point, Antonio. There is a danger that students will do that, but I believe teachers will supervise students and make sure that they are focusing on the task.

A I think teachers will find it very difficult to check on all their students. They have classes of more than 30 in some schools.

C I agree with Antonio. It'll be very difficult for teachers to monitor students. Another thing is the expense. I read that it'll cost the government over a billion pounds to introduce the Internet in all schools.

J That's not true, Carmen. The government will get local businesses to sponsor schools – so it will cost a billion – but very little of it will come from us.

C But what will happen to traditional teaching? As I see it, students will spend all their time looking at a computer screen and have very little contact with teachers.

J I don't think traditional teaching will suffer. There is a place for both.

7.9

Let me now turn to another example of green architecture and a very innovative example too. This is the World Trade Centre in Bahrain. A stunning building, I think you will agree. Completed in 2008, it is the first skyscraper in the world to have wind turbines integrated into its design.

The building in fact consists of two towers. Each is 240 metres high, which makes it the highest building in Bahrain. The towers are joined by three bridges – skybridges – and on each bridge there is attached a wind turbine – able to produce 225 kilowatts of electricity.

Each of these turbines is 29 metres in diameter – so they are very big and heavy too. Now the building is designed to face north so that the turbines also face the north. This is very important for two reasons: firstly because this is where the prevailing wind comes from, and secondly, unlike turbines fixed on the top of a tower, in wind farms for example, the position of these turbines cannot be changed. They are fixed in one position so they must face the wind.

Let's have a look at these turbines in more detail. How do they work exactly?

7.10

Another style of architecture which we should discuss is organic architecture. Now, organic architecture should not be confused with green architecture, though sometimes a building can be both. Organic architecture is architecture which takes its influence from nature and naturally-occurring figures. Unlike much of modern architecture, you see many fluid, evolving shapes and curved lines in the organic movement.

Casa Milà, a building in Barcelona, is an early example of organic architecture. Completed by the architect Antoni Gaudí in 1912, it is locally known as 'La Pedrera', or 'The Quarry' in English, because it looks like the face of a cliff where stone has been cut away. Many of the windows and doors look like caves. It is a unique space.

But there can be more to organic architecture. You see, as the buildings take their influence from nature, an organic building is usually designed to fit in well in its environment. In a city, this is not so important, but when a building is built in the countryside, or a place of natural beauty, an organic approach is often considered.

A building in America known as 'Fallingwater', designed by the architect Frank Lloyd Wright, is a good example, I think. The building is set, quite dramatically, in the middle of a forest at the top of a small waterfall. Now if you haven't seen this building, I can imagine that it sounds quite out of place. But the building makes good use of local materials. The façade – the exterior – is mostly covered in grey stone from the site and glass, which reflects views of the forest. The interior spaces are panelled with local wood. According to the architect the house allowed people to 'live with the waterfall' rather than just being able to look at it. This idea is important in organic architecture – being together 'with' nature, rather than just next to it.

8.1

Hello, welcome to another edition of *Business Now*.

Today we are looking at sports sponsorship – what is it? – and – is it a good thing for sport? The relationship between sponsorship and sport began in the USA in the 1930s when baseball became televised. Since then, it has grown dramatically and has spread all over the world and into most professional sports. In the 2010 World Cup, for example, sponsorship earned $1.6 billion for FIFA, the ruling body of world football. But who exactly benefits from this commercialization of sport? Is it good for the sponsors? What about TV companies – what profits do they get? Is it good for the sports – football, baseball, cricket, etc? Does it benefit all sportsmen and women, or only the Cristiano Ronaldos – a very successful few? And finally, what about the spectator? What do these loyal supporters get out of sponsorship?

8.2 [including 8.3]

P = Presenter   L = Leo Desa

P I put some of these questions to Leo Desa, author of the book, *The Business of Sport.* First of all I asked him for a definition. I'd like to start by asking you to define sports sponsorship. What is it exactly?

L It's actually a business relationship between – on the one hand – a provider of funds, usually a company – and on the other a sportsman or woman, such as Rafael Nadal, the tennis player. Or it could be a team or an organization such as Manchester United, which is well known around the world. So individuals and also teams can be sponsored. And we mustn't forget sporting events such as the World Cup and the Olympic Games. They can also be sponsored. Companies pay a lot of money to sponsor events like these. You may remember that FIFA, the world football ruling body, made $1.6 billion from sponsorship for the 2010 World Cup through companies such as Nike, Hyundai, Visa, Coca Cola, etc.

P Hmm. So sponsoring these major events seems to be a very expensive business. That leads me to my next question. What exactly do these companies get out of this sponsorship? It's not a form of charity, is it?

L No, it is certainly not charity. Sponsorship is really marketing – sports marketing. It combines advertising, sales promotion and public relations. Advertising is getting the brand name recognized – and of course some of these events have huge audiences – sometimes billions of people. Hopefully this translates itself into sales and profits. Public relations is important too. People all around the world like events such as the World Cup or the Olympics – in fact they like sport in general. So it is good for a company's image to be seen supporting these popular events.

P Which sports attract the most sponsorship?

L It depends on which part of the world you're talking about. In the USA, baseball and basketball attract the biggest sponsorship. In the Indian subcontinent, it is cricket. Motor racing, especially Formula One, is popular internationally in many countries. And of course there is football. Football is the most popular international sport and attracts a huge amount of money. Sponsors pay a lot to be associated with successful teams, such as Inter Milan, and also big competitions – like the World Cup, which I mentioned earlier. They also sponsor local football leagues – like the Premiership in the UK, which is sponsored by Barclays Bank. Also football stadiums such as the Emirates stadium in London are also sponsored.

[8.3 starts] P Now I'd like to turn to the question of the effect of sponsorship on sports. Has it all been beneficial? A good thing for sport?

L Well, on the positive side, it has brought money into several popular sports. This has meant that facilities can be improved – better stadiums, for example. And more people can see the sports through TV deals. It has raised standards in the sport. If a team has more money, it will attract better players and so the standard of the team should be higher. Also, if individual sportsmen and women are sponsored, they may be able to give up work so they can concentrate on their sport – running, golf, tennis, etc.

P OK, that's the positive side of sponsorship but what about the downside? A lot of people say that commercialization has ruined many sports.

L Yes, a lot of people say that. They don't like to see advertising around the edge of a playing field or the names of sponsors on the team shirt or on a cap. But it is an exaggeration to say that these sports have been ruined. Critics also point out that sponsors just concentrate on the big sports, football, motor racing, golf, tennis, baseball, and they neglect the smaller sports – such as hockey, and athletics. I think that is true to some extent. We can see that the gap between the two is getting wider.

P Aren't sponsors becoming too powerful?

L In some sports, yes, they want to change the times that sports are played, and in the case of cricket for example, they want to change the rules of the game, so that the game becomes more entertaining. By doing this they hope to attract more spectators to the stadiums and also to get a bigger TV audience.

P Isn't that a good thing?

L On the whole I think it is, but sponsors have to be careful that they don't change the game too much. And finally, some sports become too dependent on sponsorship, so if they lose their sponsors, then the sport can go into decline.

P So to conclude, Leo, what is the future of sports sponsorship? How do you see it developing in the next five, ten years?

L I think sports sponsorship will continue to grow. But the dangers are that it will focus on just a few sports or a few sports personalities. It has to be carefully controlled and we must make sure that the benefits are spread out to all sports. [8.3 ends]

8.4

Have you ever wondered what makes a champion? In today's talk I want to look at the possible reasons that some sportsmen or women perform better than others. I'll be looking at the following factors: physiology – how the body works best, nutrition – what to eat and when if you want to do well in sports, sports technology – the equipment that is used in sports and training, performance analysis – that is studying what good sportsmen do and finally, psychology – what role psychological factors play. By the end of the lecture we will know what it takes to be the perfect champion.

8.5

Let's begin with physiology. It can be described as the study of how an athlete's body works – especially as it approaches the limits – the limits of what a person is able to do when running, jumping, swimming and so on. So basically, the more we can learn about the body the more we can help athletes. We can help them to train – but also to improve their performances – to run faster, to jump higher, and so on.

Now a second important factor is nutrition. Nutrition means the food and drink we put into the athlete's body. What food and drink works best for the athlete – and when is the best time to eat and drink – and how much? Questions like these. Nutrients can be broken down into three classes: fats, carbohydrates and proteins. It is generally thought that carbohydrates – foods like rice, potatoes, pasta – are the main source of fuel for athletes.

The next factor is sports technology – the type of equipment, for example, shoes for a runner and racquets for tennis players. A lot of research goes into improving sports equipment. Let's take the tennis racquet as an example. Originally these were made of wood, but later, in order to make racquets stronger, other materials were used – first steel and later aluminium. Today they are made of a mixture of carbon fibre, fibreglass and metals such as titanium. So that's just one example of how science has been used to improve the equipment that is used by sportsmen and women.

Let's move on to another area of scientific research – performance analysis. This is an area of Sports Science that helps sportspeople and their coaches improve performance by providing a record of performance – usually using statistical information and video. This evidence is then used to evaluate and improve performance. Does it work? Yes, research shows that providing athletes with accurate feedback, based on systematic and objective analysis, is a key factor in improving sporting performance.

A final factor is that of psychology. Sports psychology is the study of the psychological factors that affect performance in sport, exercise, and physical activity. It deals with increasing performance by managing emotions and minimizing the psychological effects of injury and poor performance. Some of the most important skills taught are setting goals, relaxation techniques, visualization, concentration, and confidence.

🔊 8.6

To conclude, top athletes don't become champions by chance – or through luck. They work hard at it, day after day, through training and exercising. But in addition to this they get help from science. As I have mentioned, science helps them in a number of ways – it tells them how to move their bodies, it tells them how to train and exercise, and what equipment to use. It also tells them about nutrition – what they should eat and drink – and when. Finally, it helps them to be mentally ready for sporting events. It is a combination of these factors that leads to sporting success and produces champions.

🔊 8.7

A Hello … er … Mr … er … Tendulka.

B Chakrabati, actually.

A Oh, yes, yes, Mr Tendulka is next after you. Can you tell me something about your company, Mr Chakrabati? When was it founded?

B In 1957, in London.

A How many stores do you have now?

B Over 4,000.

A What about sports sponsorship? Do you sponsor sport?

B Yes, we do.

A What sports?

B Football. We have a contract with a team in the English Premier League.

A But according to my notes, you sponsor cricket.

B No, that was a few years ago. That contract came to an end in 2008 and since then we have only sponsored football.

A Hello, Mr Chakrabati, very pleased to meet you. My name's Jason Brown.

B How do you do, Mr Brown?

A Thank you so much for agreeing to be interviewed. As I said in my letter we are working on a project on the relationship between business and sport. First of all I'd like to get some background information on your company and then later I'd like to look at sports sponsorship in more detail.

B That's fine.

A I've been reading about your company. Could you tell me a bit about the history – the early days?

B Well, it was founded in 1957, in London as a food importer. We started with just one major store but by 1980 we had fifty stores, mainly supermarkets in the south of England and, by the year 1990 we had more than 400 stores all over the country.

A And now I believe the number is more than 4,000?

B Yes, that's right and that includes several overseas supermarkets in the Middle East, Europe and Asia.

A That's very impressive!

🔊 8.8

How many people here play tennis? Hmm – just one or two. How many people like to watch tennis on TV? Oh, quite a few! And how many people hate tennis? Only one! Good, because today I'm going to be talking about tennis – in particular about tennis racquets. I'll be looking at the way science has changed the shape of the racquets we use to play tennis. I'll start off by looking at the very first tennis racquets – big, heavy, wooden racquets that weighed a tonne. Then I'm going to look at the first metal racquets and what a technological breakthrough they were – steel and later aluminium racquets. After that, I will look in some detail at modern racquets – and how science has played a part in creating strong and very light racquets using a mixture of carbon, fibreglass and some metals. Lastly, I will be asking the question, 'What about the future of tennis racquets?' How far can science go in producing the perfect racquet?

🔊 8.9

P = Presenter   D = Darren

P Hi again from the Sports Business Outlook podcast. Today we're discussing sponsorship with Darren Lewis, Director of Marketing at All-Pro, the sports clothing company. Hello and welcome, Darren. I'd like to start by asking you about the benefits of sponsorship for your company?

D Well, I think most marketing people in our industry would agree that sponsoring professional athletes and having them publicly endorse products is quite essential really. We want to sell our line of sports clothing to people who do sport, and if those people see the professional athletes that they admire, wearing our brand of clothing, that is very good publicity for us.

P Could we turn to the question of how you decide which athletes you would like to sponsor?

D Obviously it's important that the athletes we sponsor are successful. We want to be associated with the winners. But there's actually more to it than just that. We often look for athletes who have a certain image. It helps if they're good-looking or have a lot of charisma, generally the kind of person that people want to be like.

P OK, well that's sponsoring individuals, but could we move on to the sponsorship of whole teams and clubs.

D Well, sponsoring teams has even more advantages – a larger audience who will see our logo, access to more athletes, side benefits like free tickets to matches, which we can pass on to clients. But of course, there's usually a lot more money involved than with individuals.

P Yes, well that sort of leads me to my final question. What do you think are some of the risks involved in sponsoring athletes?

D Well, there are definitely risks involved. If an athlete has a serious injury and has to stop playing after a company has invested a lot of money in them, it's bad for both the athlete and the company. Or sometimes, even worse, if the athlete is involved in some kind of a scandal – marital problems, or legal issues – if an athlete is involved in these kinds of things, that can reflect badly on the sponsor and damage the reputation of the brand.

🔊 9.1

C = Chris   CR = Charles Robertson   YM = Yuki Masaoka

C In today's discussion we're looking at trends in population growth rates – the overall picture today as well as likely trends in the future. We'll also be discussing the possible factors involved in the rise or fall of population in countries or regions. I'm joined by Dr Charles Robertson and Professor Yuki Masaoka, both researchers in the field of demographic change. Dr Robertson, could we start with you, please? What does recent population data tell us?

CR I think what we see from current statistics is that, generally speaking, the world population is continuing to grow but at a slower rate. We are currently at just under 7 billion and most estimates suggest that this figure will increase to somewhere between 8 and 10.5 billion by the year 2050. At the moment, population is increasing at around 1.1% per annum, but this rate of growth is below the peak of the 1960s when it was over 2% per annum.

C This rate of growth is not spread evenly over the world, is it? Professor Masaoka?

YM No. What we see if we look at a map of the world is that there is a wide variation in growth rates. Some regions tend to have a very high growth rate, for example sub-Saharan Africa, while other regions such as Europe have a growth rate that is much lower – for example, near zero in Germany and Italy.

C Why is there this variation – by region or by country?

YM The picture is quite complicated and there are a number of factors involved. For example, if everyone stayed in their own country then the population growth rate would just be a reflection of births and deaths in the country. This is called the natural growth rate. However, people don't stay at home. For one reason or another, a significant number of people move to other countries – for work, for study, or maybe as refugees escaping from war or economic hardship. So migration has to be taken into account to give the complete picture – this is called the overall growth rate.

C   So these factors – births, deaths, and migration – are reflected in the growth rates for these countries?

YM   That's right. Of course there are other factors involved, such as the standard of health care in a country, the effects of diseases such as malaria, wars, natural disasters and so on. These are the reasons why some countries have low birth rates and others have high birth rates – and also why death rates vary from country to country.

CR   If we look at Asia, for example, we see quite an interesting picture. In the Middle East, in countries such as Oman and Yemen, the population growth rates tend to be high. That is mainly due to a high birth rate. In the countries of Eastern Asia the growth rates tend to be lower. I could mention South Korea and Japan specifically. There are probably many reasons for this, but it seems that people generally want to have smaller families. We can see across Russia and into several Eastern European countries that the population is actually declining.

C   Is that a bad thing?

CR   Yes, because a declining population generally means an ageing population – more old people and fewer young people – and that of course has economic consequences.

C   But there are exceptions to this picture in Europe.

YM   Yes, look at France and the UK for example. Here the population growth rates are a bit higher – higher than in Germany anyway. This is probably due to a number of factors. One is net immigration – the number of people entering the country is greater than the number of people leaving. Another factor could be that, on the whole, immigrants to these countries are likely to have more children.

CR   We mustn't forget when we look at population statistics that there are other factors that influence change – hidden factors or factors that we might not expect. For example, a recent study showed that in India the birth rate falls when cable television is introduced to a village.

C   So it is quite a complex picture. Now I'd like to move onto the question of why this study of population is important. Professor?

YM   Governments need this data in order to plan for the future. They need to plan for their healthcare system, the education system, likely energy consumption and so on. So predictions about the growth of the population are very important. And if there is an ageing population as Dr Robertson mentioned, then this has implications too. There will be fewer people of working age and more retired people to support.

C   Finally, let's come back to world population. What do you think is likely to happen in the future? Can the world's population really continue to rise at this rate, because surely it is quite unsustainable? Surely it can only lead to depletion of resources and perhaps wide-scale famine?

YM   At the moment we see two trends – the world population is rising but the birth rate throughout the world is falling, as families, on average, seem to want fewer children. And sooner or later if this trend in birth rates continues the world population is likely to fall later in the 21st century, perhaps as early as 2040.

C   That's an interesting conclusion – but it could be quite a long way in the future before we see a decline.

9.2

1   Some regions tend to have a very high growth rate – for example Sub-Saharan Africa.

2   However, people don't stay at home – for one reason or another, a significant number of people move to other countries.

3   In the Middle East, in countries such as Oman and Yemen, the population growth rates tend to be high. That is mainly due to a high birth rate.

4   There are probably many reasons for this – but it seems that people generally want to have smaller families.

5   Another factor could be that, on the whole, immigrants to these countries are likely to have more children.

6   At the moment we see two trends – the world population is rising but the birth rate throughout the world is falling as families, on average, seem to want fewer children.

7   And sooner or later if this trend in birth rates continues the world population is likely to fall later in the 21st century, perhaps as early as 2040.

9.3

Good morning. Today I want to continue with a talk in our series on world trends. Before I begin, let me ask you all a question – how are you, everybody? OK, most people said 'fine' or 'OK'. No, what I really mean is how ARE you? How is your life? Are you in good health? Are you satisfied with your life? Are you achieving your goals? Can you pay your bills? Are you happy? All of these things go towards 'quality of life'. So, again … how ARE you, really? Oh, not so good! What I want to do is to look at quality of life around the world – is it getting better for most people? And, by the way, what do we mean by quality of life and how can we measure it?

So I'll start off by looking at a common measure of quality of life. It's called the Human Development Index – or HDI. I'll look at the global picture – where are the countries with a high HDI? And I'll be discussing the trends over recent years. And finally, I want to look at what opponents of the HDI say and then some of the alternative measures of quality of life. So let's get going.

9.4

The Human Development Index, or HDI, is one of the most common measures of quality of life. This was launched in 1990 by the United Nations Development Programme. Before then the emphasis when discussing human development had been on income. But the aim of the HDI was to shift the emphasis towards other factors.

Broadly speaking, there are three dimensions to the HDI: health, knowledge, and standard of living. The first, health. This is measured by life expectancy – can people expect to have a long and healthy life? Secondly, access to knowledge. This is measured by the average years of schooling that children have or can expect to have, and thirdly, a decent standard of living. This is measured by the Gross National Income per capita, how much people earn in other words. The figures are collected for each country and converted by a mathematical formula to an index – a number from 0 to 1. So, 1 is high and 0 is low.

So which countries have a high HDI? Which countries come out on top? If we look at the information in this table we can see that Norway, Australia and New Zealand occupy the top three places. They have indexes of 0.938, 0.937 and 0.907 respectively – that's the data for 2010 by the way. Countries with an HDI of 0.8 of more are considered to be 'high development' countries. At the other extreme, countries with an HDI below 0.5 are considered to be 'low development'.

If you look at the graph, HDI trends between 1975 and 2005, you can see changes in HDI by regions of the world. We can notice two things straight away: firstly, each region has a different level of HDI – the line at the top in black, for example, shows the states of the OECD – the Organization for Economic Co-operation and Development – which includes most of the European Union, the United States and other countries, up from around 0.83 in 1975 to over 0.9 in 2004. And this green line in the middle here shows the Arab states – up from around 0.54 in 1980 to nearly 0.7 by

2004. Secondly, we can also see that overall there seems to be a steady increase in the index for all of the regions – OECD here, the Arab states here – East Asia here. There are however a couple of exceptions – Sub-Saharan Africa, this line here at the bottom. You will notice that towards the end of the period the increase in this region was only slight, whereas in the other regions, especially at the end of the period, the increase was substantial. Look at South Asia. It began with roughly the same HDI as Sub-Saharan Africa in 1975 but by 2004 it was well ahead – around 0.6. The other exception is Central and Eastern Europe – represented by this line here. For a few years after 1990 there was a sharp fall in the HDI, but since 1995 the index has been rising steadily.

What about predictions for the future? Good news! Figures suggest that this improvement in HDI will continue – in all regions of the world.

Now the index has been criticized on a number of grounds. Some people say that there is no ecological consideration – looking at the country's effect on the world ecosystem. Others question the scale – and that a scale of 0 to 1 gives very little room for improvement – especially for countries at the top end of the scale. And thirdly others say there is no spiritual or moral component – the index mainly concentrates on material well-being. A radical alternative has been suggested – instead of concentrating on Gross Domestic Product or Gross Domestic Income we should consider the Gross Domestic Happiness of a country. 'How happy are people in a country?' This is the question I tried to ask all of you at the beginning. Of course, how we can measure Gross Domestic Happiness is another matter.

9.5

1 I'd like to look at some numbers to put things into perspective. This chart shows the number of students from Spain and Turkey attending the Park Lane Language School in each of the last ten years. Overall, there has been a steady increase in the number of students during this period. There was, however, a slight fall in the number of students from Spain in 2006. This might have been due to early signs of the financial crisis. However if we look at the number of Turkish students, we can see that there was no drop at this time, which is surprising.

2 The results of our survey indicate that when school is in session, students tend to use their free time for either watching TV or for sport. Now, if you look at this table you can see that during the semester only a few students said they read newspapers or magazines in their free time compared to television and sport activities. It is likely that most students get their information from the Internet and so the habit of reading is declining. The results for free time in the holidays seem to indicate that students participate in a wider variety of activities during this time. On the whole, during holidays exercise is down, and visits to family or friends is up.

9.6

1 Since 1995 there has been a rapid increase in tourists visiting Belisla. However, there was a slight fall in 2008 due to bad weather in the holiday areas.

2 Graph 2 shows a strong correlation between the number of student visa applications and the school holidays. It's clear that students apply for visas when they are on school holidays because that's when they have the free time to do it.

3 The bar chart shows that five students usually work at home, two in the library, two in the computer lab and one outside. Therefore we can say that 50% of students prefer to study in their own homes, while only 10% study outside.

4 Sales of four-wheel drives increased sharply between 2010 and 2011 while sales of saloon cars fell slightly.

9.7

A We took a random sample of people shopping in the mall, male and female, young and old. Altogether we interviewed 50 people over a weekend. We decided to choose a weekend as we thought that there would be more young people in the mall at that time and we wanted to get a broad range of ages. We devised a questionnaire with a total of 15 questions. We wanted to include smokers in the survey group, so the first question we asked was to find out if they smoked.

B So to sum up, the aim of our survey was to find out what the attitude of people shopping in malls was to smoking in the malls. Our results tend to show that most people are greatly affected by smoke, and would support a ban. Even some smokers supported a ban. Around a third of our survey group didn't support a ban but thought that there should be areas set aside in the mall where people could smoke. What conclusions can we draw from the findings? In our view, the best solution was to set aside a special smoking area. Although just over 50% supported a ban, we feel this majority was not large enough to justify a complete ban.

C I'd like to start by asking a few questions. Firstly, how many people here like to visit shopping malls? Hmm. I see most of you. And how many of you find you are disturbed by people smoking inside the malls? About half. Well, in our survey we wanted to find out what people thought about smoking in malls – if it should be restricted – or if it should be banned. As you may know, there is now a substantial body of evidence which appears to show that passive smoking can be a cause of respiratory diseases and cancer and is especially dangerous for small children. As a result, smoking restrictions are being imposed in many situations, for example public transport and the workplace. We wanted to know if the majority of the public felt the restrictions should be extended to other public places.

D As you can see from the pie chart, half of our group were male and half were female. The ages of the group ranged from 16 to 80. And about a quarter of our survey group were smokers. When we asked the question 'How are you affected by smoke in shopping malls?' about 38% said they were greatly affected – and only 23% said they were not affected. It's interesting to point out that even some smokers didn't like the effects of people smoking in the shopping malls. When we asked about solutions to the problem, about 61% supported an outright ban on smoking in malls, as you can see from this table here.

9.8

So, we can see from this map that the area of highest population density is really focused in the north and centre of the continent – the Netherlands, Germany – the UK a bit to the west, though you can see from these light green areas that there is less density from Switzerland down through the Balkans. The countries to the east are also less crowded. The Scandinavian countries, to the far north, here, are in beige, as the climate there makes large regions of those countries less habitable.

9.9

OK, as you can see from the title of this slide, we're discussing the Human Poverty Index. Now the Human Poverty Index was developed by the United Nations as another way of showing 'standard of living'. It's quite similar to the Human Development Index we discussed, but is primarily used with developed countries, countries which are industrialized and have higher incomes, though of course this definition is open for debate.

The criteria that the Human Poverty Index uses are a long and healthy life, knowledge and a decent standard of living. At the top of the list are countries which have very low poverty, according to this set of criteria, for example, Sweden, Norway and The Netherlands. This next slide shows how the data breaks down for Sweden. So, as you can see, the percentage of people who won't live to be 60 years old is 6.7. The second figure down – 7.5 – is the percentage of people lacking functional literacy skills, and functional literacy skills just means the ability to read and write and communicate. And the final figure shows long-term unemployment, which in Sweden is a very low 1.1.

10.1

S = Sue

S   Welcome to *Technology Input*. I'm Sue Parker and today's topic is e-publishing. Today we're in Hong Kong, looking at a new e-book service offered by a Hong Kong-based publishing company, Chance Publishing.
Chance Publishing has just launched a new publishing project – an e-book list. It means that readers can now download the latest books to their phones, computers, PDAs, and e-book readers. But in addition to books, the reader can also download other media content related to the book – for example, videos, pictures, music, and computer games. Some people say that this is the future of publishing. Now this is the question I want to explore. Does everyone really gain from e-publishing? Here is Jamie Lee, the Managing Director of the company, to explain.

10.2

J = Jamie   S = Sue

J   I believe we are offering two things that are new. First we're introducing the latest books written by our own authors. So we are not just offering books that were written long ago – classics, for example – we're supplying readers with recent books. And secondly, we are offering multi-media with the book. This means that the reader can download books that are embedded with other media content – such as videos, pictures, music, games and so on. So it's a complete package. In my opinion, it makes the reading experience much more rewarding. Imagine reading a novel and also having pictures or a short video or an audio soundtrack to go alongside it. It's an altogether much more interesting experience.

S   So the claim is that this e-publishing service gives the reader a more interesting experience. But what about e-readers in general? Do these devices – phones, e-readers, laptops, etc. – represent the future of reading?

J   There'll still be people who like the traditional book for a number of reasons. Firstly, they say they love traditional books and why should they change their habits? But if a book lover has, say 200 books, then that represents a lot of space in someone's home or office. Now imagine if those 200 books could all be on an easy-to-carry e-reader. Travelling or moving home would also be a lot easier. A second point that is brought up is the question of reading text from a screen. A lot of people say they don't like to read in this way because there's too much glare. They find that looking at the bright light of the screen hurts the eyes, but modern screens have advanced a lot. Tests show that they're much easier on the eye – and the glare is reduced. Many e-readers nowadays incorporate e-ink, which is specially designed for electronic readers and has less glare than the traditional LCD screen. So I believe there will still be a market for traditional books and the two forms will exist side by side. But increasingly, I think e-books will take over a substantial sector of the publishing business. You only have to look at the sales figures.

S   Well, publishers seem happy with e-books but what about authors? What do they think about this innovation? And what do they think about the videos and soundtracks that go with the book?

J   It's true that a few authors are worried about this innovation, but, in fact from my own research, I find that most authors actually welcome this change. They don't see it as a threat. They see it as a challenge – a new way of being creative by using sound, and still or moving pictures with their books. They say, 'This is wonderful – it means we can do anything we want!'

S   Let's look at the music industry for a moment. They were in a similar position a few years ago when the downloading of music from the Internet really began. Can we learn anything from the way the music industry responded to the situation?

J   The music industry is an example of what the publishing industry should not do. As you know, the music industry was very much against the downloading of music – at least in the beginning. And some people say, 'Why should the book publishing business be different? Shouldn't they try to stop it too?' Well, as I see it the music industry made a big mistake. Instead of embracing – welcoming – a new market, they tried to stop it. And of course they failed. Downloading music was too popular amongst the public, especially young people. I really believe we should learn from the mistakes that the music industry made. The publishing industry has been in slow decline for some time now, at least in some areas of publishing. Therefore we should welcome the e-book and the new technology. It's a new market and it will bring a whole new group of people back to reading and that's good for everyone!

10.3

Each year *Technology Review* selects what it believes are the most important emerging technologies. The winners are chosen by the editors to cover key fields. The question we ask is simple: is the technology likely to change the world? Some of these changes are on the largest possible scale: better biofuels, more efficient solar cells and green concrete all aim to tackle global warming in the years ahead. Other changes are more local and involve how we use technology: for example, 3D screens on mobile devices, new applications for cloud computing and social television. New ways to implant medical electronics will affect us all and promise to make our lives healthier.

What I'd like to do in today's lecture, the last in this semester on technology, is to briefly review five of the selected technologies – new technologies that may become important in the near future. The five examples we have selected come from five different fields – from communication, construction, medicine, science and lastly the media.

10.4

1   The winners are chosen by the editors to cover key fields. The question we ask is simple: is the technology likely to change the world?

2   Some of these changes are on the largest possible scale: better biofuels, more efficient solar cells and green concrete all aim to tackle global warming in the years ahead.

3   Other changes are more local and involve how we use technology: for example 3D screens on mobile devices, new applications for cloud computing and social television.

4   What I'd like to do in today's lecture, the last in this semester on technology, is to briefly review five of the selected technologies – new technologies that may become important in the near future.

5   The five examples we have selected come from five different fields – from communication, construction, medicine, science and lastly the media.

10.5

Let's begin with communication and the way we go about looking for information. Today an increasing amount of information comes in streams – that is to say continuous data – coming from Twitter, Facebook, blogs and news outlets. Search engines such as Google are now trying to make use of this continuous source of information in the same way as they search the usual websites. This process is known as Real Time Search. Real Time Search is still developing but looks as though it has an important role to play in the future.

The next innovation I want to look at is solar fuel. Scientists are working on ways of using microbes instead of crops to produce fuel.

These microbes do not require a lot of water and they do not need good quality agricultural land. The result would be an advanced biofuel – or solar fuel – and this could mean a revolution in fuel production.

Now I'd like to look at another interesting innovation – green concrete. The production of cement for concrete, as you know, involves heating a mixture of limestone, clay, and sand using a fuel, such as coal or gas. This process generates a lot of carbon dioxide. Now what if we could change the process so that the cement absorbs more carbon dioxide than it releases? This is what scientists in London have done. By using magnesium in the production of cement, carbon dioxide is actually taken in by the cement.

The selection in the field of medicine is implantable electronics. Implants have been used for some time in surgery. These small electronic devices are placed inside a person's body where they can control a function of the body – for example, a pacemaker is placed in the heart to make it work better. The problem with these devices is that they have to be removed at some point – which means more surgery. One possible solution to this problem is the use of silk to make these implants. Silk is a soft material and is also biodegradable – it breaks down. That means the implant will dissolve over a period of time and disappear. Therefore, there is no need to remove the device from the body.

Finally, a technology which combines two media, social networking and television. Television has traditionally been a very passive activity. Basically, we sit on a sofa, we watch. As a result, television viewing has been declining in many parts of the world as more and more people spend their time on other activities such as the Internet and computer games. But social TV aims to make TV more interactive – so that the person sitting on the sofa is more involved. It combines social networking – tweets, Facebook, etc. – with TV. The viewers can easily find programmes to watch and share, and discuss the content with others.

🔊 10.6

1 Our course starts next week and ends in January.
2 The results showed that Osman was rather weak in Maths and Physics.
3 A note was made of the weight of the substance before and after heating.
4 The committee decided to wait for the report before making a decision.
5 The airport terminal was constructed using mainly glass and steel.
6 If a student plagiarizes a text then they really steal the author's ideas.
7 The principal aim of the presentation is to outline changes in book technology.
8 An important principle of chemistry is that it is better to prevent waste than to clean it up afterwards.
9 The site of the new airport will be decided by the government next year.
10 The sight of so many people in the crowded shopping mall made Sami feel claustrophobic.

🔊 10.7

A I think that e-books are just a passing fashion and in a few years they will be forgotten. I love paper books. I like to hold them and read them. Most people I know agree. A friend of mine bought one of these e-readers but after a couple of weeks she put it back in the box. She didn't like using it and now she reads ordinary books. I hate reading from screens – I haven't tried e-readers but I use computers all the time and I hate reading from the screen.
B I personally don't like using e-books. I have tried using an e-reader, and I agree that some of the features are useful, but I

wouldn't want to buy one. I admit that the sales of some e-readers are impressive, but I wonder how long this will last. Interestingly, a recent survey of young people showed that young people prefer books when it comes to reading. It is true that online newspapers are very popular. But at the moment most of these newspapers are free. What will happen when readers have to pay?

🔊 10.8

A Today's talk is going to be about iPads. The iPad is a tablet computer designed and developed by Apple. It is particularly marketed as a platform for audio and visual media such as books, periodicals, movies, music, and games, as well as Web content. It weighs about 700 grams, so its size and weight are between those of most modern smartphones and laptop computers. Apple released the iPad in April 2010, and sold 3 million of the devices in 80 days.
B Today's talk is about green concrete. Concrete is a familiar substance. Its durable nature and versatile applications have made its usage ubiquitous throughout our cities. However, this primary building material is also extremely energy-intensive to make and transport, and produces a significant amount of the world's greenhouse gas emissions. Can the omnipresent grey substance ever be reconciled as a green building material?
C Hello. I'm going to talk today about smartphones and I have a slide of a smartphone – just a minute – sorry – not that one – yes, there. As you can see it's just like a mobile phone – but it has extra functions, for example – it has advanced computer ability. So it's a bit like a computer that you can hold in your hand. About 45 million people have a smartphone – 45 million. Oh, that's just in the USA – I expect it's more in the rest of the world – in fact, I can show you the sales of smartphones on this chart – sorry – this chart.

🔊 10.9

Another industry that is going through a period of change is the film industry. And the technology I'm talking about here is not used in the production of films. I'm not going to talk about CGI or 3D technologies, though those are undoubtedly changing film as well. No, rather I'm going to focus on methods of distribution, by which I mean, how film companies deliver films to home audiences.

There have been quite a few innovations over the years in the home video market. VHS went out in favour of higher quality DVDs in the late 1990s. Now at the moment, you can still find DVDs in rental shops, but a number of large rental chains have gone out of business recently. This is partially due to the popularity of services where customers order DVDs online and receive them in the mail. Then, after they've viewed the film, they mail the DVD back in the enclosed envelope. It's easy, and cheaper than renting a video from a shop, but even this distribution method seems to be nearing its end. The problem is that in the age of the Internet, mail services are too slow for consumers. Sites like iTunes and Youtube have made it seem normal for us to get content instantly. Thanks to new faster Internet technologies like fibre-optic cables, online video streaming is now available in many places. Online streaming lets you watch your desired film online, instantly. There are several subscription services available, where you pay a certain price each month, and then you can watch unlimited films. I think this pricing system, in addition to the convenience, will appeal to many consumers. I think it's quite probable that we'll see less and less physical media – like DVDs – in the coming years.

Photocopiable Speaking Activities

Contents

Take the floor *Could I just make a point?*	Take the floor *I'd like to add something here...*	Take the floor *I agree with_____, but I'd just like to say...*	Take the floor *Could I say something here?*	Take the floor *Yes, but...*
Hold the floor *Could you just hold on?*	Hold the floor *Could I just finish?*	Hold the floor *Well, let me explain...*	Hold the floor *Sorry, but I'd just like to finish by saying...*	Hand over *What does everyone else think?*
Hand over *Does everyone agree?*	Hand over *_____, what do you think?*	Hand over *Would you like to comment, _____?*	Hand over *_____, what do you think?*	Hand over *Would you like to comment, _____?*
Take the floor *Could I just make a point?*	Take the floor *I'd like to add something here...*	Take the floor *I agree with_____, but I'd just like to say...*	Take the floor *Could I say something here?*	Take the floor *Yes, but...*
Hold the floor *Could you just hold on?*	Hold the floor *Could I just finish?*	Hold the floor *Well, let me explain...*	Hold the floor *Sorry, but I'd just like to finish by saying...*	Hand over *What does everyone else think?*
Hand over *Does everyone agree?*	Hand over *_____, what do you think?*	Hand over *Would you like to comment, _____?*	Hand over *_____, what do you think?*	Hand over *Would you like to comment, _____?*
TOPIC Which is more important in language learning: linguistic intelligence or hard work and practice?	TOPIC Which is more important in business: logical-mathematical or interpersonal intelligence?	TOPIC What academic subjects require a lot of spatial intelligence?	TOPIC Can you think of some examples of people who have high bodily-kinaesthetic intelligence?	TOPIC How could you use musical intelligence to study vocabulary?
TOPIC What is the difference between interpersonal intelligence and intrapersonal intelligence?	TOPIC If you could have more of one of the seven intelligences, which would you choose?	TOPIC Is there enough evidence to support the theory of multiple intelligences?	TOPIC Which is the most important of the intelligences mentioned in the unit?	TOPIC Are there other types of intelligence besides the seven mentioned in the unit?

Student A

Work with a partner. Read the information in the outlines below to give an introduction to a talk about a study, while your partner takes notes. Then listen as your partner gives an introduction, and record the information in the box on the right.

The importance of sleep by Dr. Adrianne Hammer Survey results: • Most people sleep less than 6 hours per night. • 80% of people can't sleep at least once a week. • 50% of people feel tired all day. Advantages of getting enough sleep: • Increases memory. • Better metabolism (the way the body uses food). • Easier weight management. • Decreased risk of heart disease. • Helps fight cancer. • Injuries heal faster. Advice to patients: • Try to get 7–9 hours of sleep per night. • Do not watch television or use the computer before bed. • Check with your doctor if you have sleep apnea (breathing problems during sleep).	Name of speaker: _____ Topic of speech: _____ Definition of terms: _____ Reasons for study: _____ Aim/objective: _____ Opinion: _____ Plan: _____ 1 _____ 2 _____ 3 _____

Student B

Work with a partner. Listen as your partner gives an introduction, and record the information in the box on the right. Then read the information in the outline below to give an introduction to a talk about a study, while your partner takes notes.

Vitamin D by Dr. Patricia Spinner Introduction: • Vitamin D is a fat-soluble vitamin. • Comes in two forms: D2 and D3. Studies about Vitamin D: • 50% of women may not have enough Vitamin D. • Experts disagree about how much is enough. • People with high body fat need more Vitamin D. Advantages of Vitamin D: • Reduces risk of breast cancer, heart disease, and diabetes. • May prevent depression and weight gain. • Helps the body build bones and muscles. • Prevents bone problems like osteoporosis. Sources of Vitamin D: • 30 minutes of sunlight exposure, twice per week. • Food: fish, eggs and cheese. • Supplements (pills).	Name of speaker: _____ Topic of speech: _____ Definition of terms: _____ Reasons for study: _____ Aim/objective: _____ Opinion: _____ Plan: _____ 1 _____ 2 _____ 3 _____

Speaking 3 Organizing a presentation: Urban planning

Student A

Read the nine statements. Organize them into Introduction, Body, and Conclusion. Then use the notes to give a short talk to your classmates.

a	According to a study in 2002, people were willing to walk between 0.5 km and 1 km to get to a park.
b	First, urban planners must consider how far apart to locate the parks.
c	I'm Dr. Paula Robin, professor of Urban Planning studies.
d	This distance depends on factors like safety, the beauty of the neighbourhood, and the climate of the city.
e	This means, if urban planners want to increase the value of the land in the city, they should put a park every 2 km.
f	Title: Putting parks in cities
g	To do this, they look at how far people are willing to walk to get to a park.
h	Today, we'll examine how urban planners plan parks in cities.
i	Tomorrow, we'll look at the next step in planning parks. Are there any questions?

Student B

Read the nine statements. Organize them into Introduction, Body, and Conclusion. Then use the notes to give a short talk to your classmates.

a	All of these solutions could reduce our traffic problem. I recommend that we use a combination of them.
b	Another idea is to improve bus lines and reduce the costs of the bus.
c	Finally, some people feel that we should make all drivers pay an extra fee to own a car in the city.
d	Hello, my name is Asma Aziz. I'm the president of Aziz Urban Planning and Development Group.
e	In this talk, I will outline a few of the solutions that urban planners have created to deal with this issue.
f	One solution is to add tolls to the busiest roads in the city. People would rather take a different road than pay.
g	Title: Too much traffic!
h	Traffic is an important issue nowadays. Many cities are reaching the point where there are too many cars.
i	We seem to be out of time. If there are any questions, please send me an email.

Student C

Read the nine statements. Organize them into Introduction, Body, and Conclusion. Then use the notes to give a short talk to your classmates.

a	Finally, paid parking can be a source of funds for cities, which have suffered a lot in the recent economic crisis.
b	First of all, paid parking is a way to control where people park. All-day parkers can park in free car parks.
c	Good evening. My name is Dr. Van Acker, and I'm going to talk to you about the benefits of paid parking.
d	I'd be happy to answer any questions you might have.
e	My aim in this presentation has been to show you the advantages of a paid parking system.
f	Paid parking also reduces overall traffic. People will choose to walk, or take the bus, rather than drive.
g	Paid parking is often a very unpopular choice, but it can actually help a city in several ways.
h	This leaves paid spaces in front of shops open for customers to park for short times.
i	Title: Paid parking in the city

Student D

Read the nine statements. Organize them into Introduction, Body, and Conclusion. Then use the notes to give a short talk to your classmates.

a	Another way is by creating a system of shared bicycles. People could pay monthly, and use them when needed.
b	Does anyone have a question?
c	First of all, there is too much automobile traffic here. If more people ride bikes, this will decrease.
d	Good morning. I'm Chris Wagner, from the Citizens Council for Urban Development.
e	I believe that there are three ways to make this happen. One is to put cycle paths on the side of every road.
f	I strongly recommend that you consider these ideas. Our city would benefit greatly from them.
g	My aim for this talk is to show you how important bicycles are in this city, and how we can help cyclists.
h	The third way is to offer bonuses and discounts for people who use bicycles instead of cars.
i	Title: Bicycles and urban planning

Student A

Describe Syria to your partner. Listen to your partner describe a country. Record the missing information. Then, tell your partner about Turkey. Listen to your partner describe the next country. Record the missing information.

Country	Syria		Turkey	
Location	Middle East, between Turkey and Lebanon		South-east Europe and South-west Asia	
Area	185,180 sq km		783,562 sq km	
Population	22,517,750		78,785,548	
Climate	Summers hot and dry, winters mild and rainy		Summers hot and dry, winters mild and wet	
Life expectancy	74.7 years		72.5 years	
Main industries	Petroleum, textiles		Textiles, food processing, cars	
Main crops	Chickpeas, olives, wheat		Tobacco, grain, cotton	

Student B

Listen to your partner describe a country. Record the missing information. Then, tell your partner about Bulgaria. Listen to your partner describe the next country and record the missing information. Then tell your partner about Romania.

Country		Bulgaria		Romania
Location		South-east Europe between Turkey and Romania		South-east Europe
Area		110,879 sq km		238,391 sq km
Population		7,093,635		21,904,551
Climate		Summers hot and dry, winters cold and damp		Summers rainy, winters cold and snowy
Life expectancy		73.6 years		74.0 years
Main industries		Electricity, gas, food, and beverages		Electrical machinery and equipment
Main crops		Tobacco, sunflowers, barley		Wheat, corn, barley

Work in groups. Look at the graphs below. Using your world knowledge, try to complete the missing information. You can check your answers on the Internet.

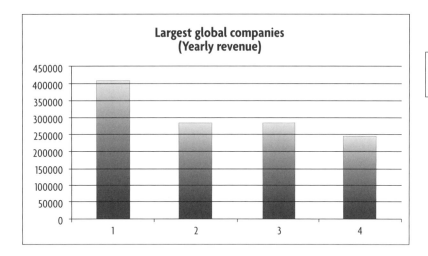

BP   Exxon Mobil   Wal-Mart Stores
Royal Dutch Shell

Germany   United States
United Kingdom   Canada   Italy
The Netherlands   France   South Korea
Japan   People's Republic of China

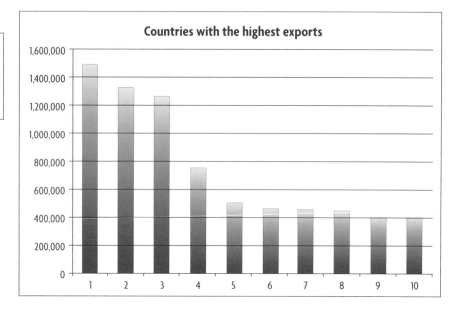

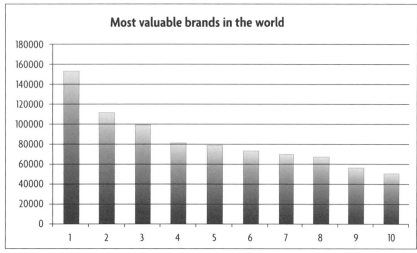

Google   China Mobile   Apple
IBM   McDonald's   Coca-Cola
AT&T   Microsoft   Marlboro
General Electric

Student A

Four people are discussing a possible heritage site in their city. Each person has a point of view and some hidden assumptions. Find them and discuss them with your group.

Hello, I'm Dr. Benjamin Marcus, from the City Conservation Committee. My aim today is to present a proposal to save the Old City Market, which is located in the city centre. Our plan may cost a lot of money, but it is worth it to conserve this valuable piece of our city's heritage. First, we will appoint experts in the field of conservation to come and assess the condition of the Old City Market. Then, we will repair the walls of the market. I would personally make sure that the materials we use for the walls will be very different from the old materials, so that everyone can clearly see which parts are the old walls, and what has been fixed. Please consider my recommendations.

Student B

Four people are discussing a possible heritage site in their city. Each person has a point of view and some hidden assumptions. Find them and discuss them with your group.

Good morning. I'm Asma Aziz, from the Aziz Urban Planning and Development Group. According to our research, this city desperately needs new parks and outdoor spaces. The Old City Market would be an excellent location for a children's park. The area around the Market is densely populated. In fact, 50% of our city's residents live within one kilometre. Currently, the state of the old walls of the Market presents a danger to children. In addition, they are profitable places for criminals to operate. If we replace the Market with an open, well-lit park, we can provide a safe place for children to play, and reduce crime at the same time. If you have any questions, please feel free to ask.

Student C

Four people are discussing a possible heritage site in their city. Each person has a point of view and some hidden assumptions. Find them and discuss them with your group.

Hello. I'm Dr. Yulia Kolpakova, Chair of the Department of Conservation at the University. I agree with Dr. Marcus that we need to save the Old City Market. However, the Market is only one of the historical sites in the city which are in urgent need of conservation. We cannot afford to spend our limited budget on the Old City Market when other sites, such as the Central Fort, are also in danger. On the outskirts of the city is an even older village which should be saved. Archaeological studies of this village could tell us even more about our history and culture. I believe this is a much more important heritage site. It could even be declared a UNESCO World Heritage site. Does anyone have any questions?

Student D

Four people are discussing a possible heritage site in their city. Each person has a point of view and some hidden assumptions. Find them and discuss them with your group.

Good afternoon. I'm Ryan Svenson from Svenson Attractions Company. I'd like to share our idea for the Old City Market. We would like to invest in the site, and create a tourist attraction for the city. We will restore the Old City Market walls, so that the Market looks exactly like it did hundreds of years ago. No one will even be able to see the difference. We will bring in small shops and vendors such as Starbucks, to open their businesses in the Market, which will attract both residents and tourists. The central square of the Market will be kept clear for events and concerts. I am certain that this development will be good for the economy of the city, and for its residents. Thank you, and feel free to ask any questions.

Work in groups. Briefly discuss each statement. Do you agree or disagree? One group member should write down the names of who agrees and who disagrees. Give reasons for your points of view. When you have finished, report back to the class.

Topics	Agree	Disagree
1 Airports are usually comfortable and relaxing places.		
2 All large buildings should use solar power.		
3 Buildings should be replaced if they are old and ugly.		
4 To keep a city beautiful, it is best not to have any buildings higher than three stories.		
5 Skyscrapers are beautiful buildings.		
6 Builders should include parking spaces with every new building.		
7 Cities full of large buildings can be better for the environment than suburbs.		
8 Sustainable building materials should always be used, no matter how much they cost.		
9 Airports should always be very large.		
10 Wind power is the best alternative energy source.		

Speaking 8 Information gap: Talking about sport as a business

Student A

Work with a partner. Ask questions to find the missing information. Compare papers to check answers.

Sport	Football	Hockey	Basketball	Motor racing	Tennis
Largest league		NHL		Formula 1	
Highest-earning event	FIFA World Cup		NBA Finals		Wimbledon
Highest product endorsement deals		$10,000,000		$25,000,000	
Highest annual salary for a player	$12,833,671		$21,000,000		$7,000,000
Average attendance per game		17,460		75,130	

Student B

Work with a partner. Ask questions to find the missing information. Compare papers to check answers.

Sport	Football	Hockey	Basketball	Motor racing	Tennis
Largest league	UK Premier League		NBA		No league
Highest-earning event		Stanley Cup		World Championship	
Highest product endorsement deals	$160,000,000		$25,000,000		$40,000,000
Highest annual salary for a player		$9,538,461		$51,000,000	
Average attendance per game	42,565		17,520		No information available

Speaking 9 Analyzing data: World trends

Student A

Describe Survey Report A to your partner. Then, while your partner describes Survey Report B, record the missing information. Compare papers to check your answers. Look at both surveys critically. How can you interpret this data?

Survey Report A

Aim: To find out how we can improve our city to attract new residents.

Method: Anonymous Internet survey. We sent out emails to random residents with a link to the survey. We received 53 responses.

Results:

What would you most like to see added to our city?

Parks for walking my dog	56%
Bike paths	28%
Green buildings	10%
Better schools	5%

What is the biggest problem in the city?

Not enough dog parks	56%
High taxes	30%
Too much traffic	16%

Survey Report B

Aim: _____

Method: _____

Results: _____

How often do you use the following at work?

Technology	Everyday	Sometimes	Never
Facebook		5%	
	30%		37%
Wikipedia	12%		
	25%	30%	45%
Online games		4%	
	90%	8%	3%

Student B

Listen as your partner describes Survey Report A and complete the missing information. Then describe Survey Report B while your partner records the information. Compare papers to check your answers. Look at both surveys critically. How can you interpret this data?

Survey Report A

Aim: _____

Method: _____
_____

Results: _____

What would you most like to see added to our city?

Parks for walking my dog	____
_____	28%
Green buildings	____
_____	5%

What is the biggest problem in the city?

Not enough dog parks	____
_____	30%
Too much traffic	____

Survey Report B

Aim: To find out how people use technology at work.

Method: Personal interviews and surveys with employees in their offices. We surveyed over 500 people in three different large companies.

Results:

How often do you use the following at work?

Technology	Everyday	Sometimes	Never
Facebook	5%	5%	90%
Databases	30%	33%	37%
Wikipedia	12%	80%	8%
Webmail	25%	30%	45%
Online games	2%	4%	94%
Word processor	90%	8%	3%

Require all schools to have computer labs.	Link TV with social networking sites like Facebook, to share data about what shows people like.	Allow people under the age of 18 to have plastic surgery.	Require computer literacy tests for all employees.	Replace all books with e-books.
Give all citizens email and Facebook accounts as soon as they finish secondary school.	Teach most courses entirely online.	Ban the Internet in schools.	Use Google, Gmail, and Google Maps for government services like taxes, gas and water bills.	Allow people to download music and films for free.
Require all cars to be hybrid or electric by the year 2020.	Implant small electronic devices in people's bodies for identification and tracking purposes.	Use computer games to teach students maths, English, and other subjects.	Make medicine free in developing countries.	Implant electronic devices to detect heart disease, diabetes, cancer, and other problems.
Give people severe punishments for driving while talking on a mobile phone.	Give everyone an e-reader in secondary school.	Require all offices to stop using paper and move to an online system.	Use only solar power in all government buildings.	Replace all radio programmes with streaming content on the Internet.
Advantage	Advantage	Advantage	Advantage	Advantage
Advantage	Advantage	Advantage	Advantage	Advantage
Advantage	Advantage	Advantage	Advantage	Advantage
Advantage	Advantage	Advantage	Advantage	Advantage
Disadvantage	Disadvantage	Disadvantage	Disadvantage	Disadvantage
Disadvantage	Disadvantage	Disadvantage	Disadvantage	Disadvantage
Disadvantage	Disadvantage	Disadvantage	Disadvantage	Disadvantage
Disadvantage	Disadvantage	Disadvantage	Disadvantage	Disadvantage

Photocopiable

1 Group discussion: Multiple Intelligences

AIM

To reinforce the Study Skill and language of Taking turns in a discussion, Student's Book, Unit 1 (p9). This is a conversation and card came. Make enough copies of the worksheet so that each group has one set of cards. Cut up the cards before the lesson.

PROCEDURE

1 Divide students into groups of 4–6.

2 Review the Language Bank on p9. Highlight the function of these phrases, and the fact that they are followed by additional information or commentary.

3 Deal out the small cards (Language Bank phrases). Make sure each student has a variety of phrases and functions.

4 The Topic cards go in the middle. The group turns over the first Topic card and begins to discuss the topic.

5 A student can 'play' one of his/her small cards by using the phrase appropriately.

6 The students continue turning over the Topic cards and discussing the new topics.

7 The first player to use all of his/her cards wins the game.

2 Introduction to a presentation: Good health

AIM

To practise the Study Skill of Introducing a presentation and reinforce the language of Introductions, Student's Book, Unit 2 (p17). This is a talking from notes activity.

PROCEDURE

1 Make enough photocopies so that each student receives either Student A's or Student B's information.

2 Review the Language Bank on p17.

3 Divide students into pairs and give each partner half of the page.

4 Give students a few minutes to look at and understand the information on the outlines, and plan their introductions.

5 Students should practise using the phrases in the Language Bank to introduce their talks.

6 As Student A gives the introduction, Student B records information from the introduction on his/her paper.

7 Then Student B gives the introduction to his/her topic and Student A records information from the introduction on his/her paper.

8 Students compare papers to check their answers.

3 Organizing a presentation: Urban planning

AIM

To reinforce the Study Skills of Organizing the content of a presentation, Student's Book, Unit 3 (p25). This is a jigsaw activity, done in groups. Make one worksheet per group of eight students. Cut up a card for each pair of students before the lesson so that students can reorganize the statements.

PROCEDURE

1 Review the Study Skill on p25 (Organizing the main content), as well as what should be in the Introduction, Body, and Conclusion of a presentation.

2 Divide students into pairs, AA, BB, CC, DD, and give each pair one of the cut-up cards.

3 Students work together, organizing the statements into notes for a talk. It helps to first identify which sentences belong in an introduction and conclusion.

4 Change groups so that each group has one Student A, B, C, D. Each student reports to the new group by giving a short talk from their notes.

5 Check the correct answers for all the cards in open class.

ANSWERS

1 f, c, h, b, g, a, d, e, i
2 g, d, h, e, f, b, c, a, i
3 i, c, g, b, h, f, a, e, d
4 i, d, g, c, e, a, h, f, b

4 Summarizing: Food, water, and energy

AIM

To reinforce the Study Skill of Describing facts and figures, Student's Book, Unit 4 (p33). This activity involves making a summary, asking questions, and note-taking. Make enough photocopies so that each student receives one of the tables.

PROCEDURE

1 Divide students into pairs, Student A and Student B.

2 Give students about 5–10 minutes to read their text quietly.

3 Review the Study Skill on p33 (Describing facts and figures).

4 First, Student A describes the information in the first column, while Student B records the missing information in the table.

5 The students then swap roles for the remaining three columns.

6 Students compare papers to check their answers.

5 Talking about charts: Global trade

AIM

To practise the Study Skills of Presenting with graphs and charts, Student's Book Unit 5 (p41). Each group receives one worksheet.

PROCEDURE

1 Divide the students into groups of 3–4.

2 Using what they have learned about cities in Unit 5, and their world knowledge, students guess where the companies, countries, and brands go on the three charts. Instruct the students to discuss the graphs.

3 Go over the answers as a class. As students share their answers, award points for groups with the correct answers.

4 Alternatively, this could be done as a research task, with students finding out the information from the Internet, encyclopaedias or other reference books.

ANSWERS

Graph 1

1 Wal-Mart Stores

2 Royal Dutch Shell

3 Exxon Mobil

4 BP

Graph 2

1 People's Republic of China

2 Germany

3 United States

4 Japan

5 France

6 South Korea

7 Italy

8 The Netherlands

9 Canada

10 United Kingdom

Graph 3

1 Apple

2 Google

3 IBM

4 McDonald's

5 Microsoft

6 CocaCola

7 AT&T

8 Marlboro

9 China Mobile

10 General Electric

6 Finding hidden assumptions: Conserving the past

AIM

To practise the Study Skills of Detecting points of view and assumptions, Student's Book, Unit 6 (p47). This is a group discussion activity. Each group has one set of cards. Cut up the cards before the lesson.

PROCEDURE

1 Review the Study Skill on p47 (Detecting points of view and assumptions).

2 Divide students into groups of four, and give each student one of the cards.

3 Give students 5–10 minutes to go over the notes and find the speaker's point of view, strong/weak arguments, and hidden assumptions.

4 Students then summarize the information to their groups.

5 After each short talk, the group should discuss the speaker's point of view, strong/weak arguments, and hidden assumptions.

6 Finally, each group should choose whose point of view makes the most sense and what should be done to the Old City Market.

7 Expressing points of view: Modern structures

AIM

To reinforce the Study Skill and language of Supporting a point of view, and Agreeing and disagreeing, Student's Book, Unit 7 (p56). This is a group discussion activity. Make one copy of the worksheet for each group of students.

PROCEDURE

1 Organize students into groups of 4–6.
2 Review the Study Skill and Language Bank on p56 (Supporting a point of view and Agreeing and disagreeing).
3 Students read and discuss each prompt, practising the phrases in the Language Bank.
4 When they have finished, students report back on the opinions stated in their discussions.

8 Information gap: Talking about sport as a business

AIM

To use the topic of Unit 8 to reinforce and revise the Study Skills of Describing facts and figures, Student's Book, Unit 4 (p33), and Summarizing data from a table, Unit 6 (p48) . This is an information gap activity.

PROCEDURE:

1 Make one copy of the worksheet for each pair of students.
2 Divide students into pairs, Student A and Student B.
3 Students ask and answer questions to complete the missing information in the tables.
4 Students compare papers to check their answers.

9 Analyzing data: World trends

AIM

To reinforce the Study Skills involved in Analyzing data critically, Student's Book, Unit 9 (p72). This is an information gap and discussion activity. Make one copy of the worksheet for each pair of students.

PROCEDURE:

1 Divide students into pairs, Student A and Student B.

2 Give students about 5–10 minutes to read their text quietly.

3 Review the Study Skill on p72 (Analyzing data critically).

4 First, Student A describes the information in the first survey report, while Student B records the missing information.

5 Then students swap roles for the next report.

6 Students compare papers to check their answers.

7 Then ask students to discuss the two studies critically. Are the studies good ones? Ask students to give reasons for their answer.

10 Building an argument: Communication and technology

AIM

To review the idea of discussing advantages and disadvantages, and to practise the language of Building an argument, Student's Book, Unit 10 (p80). This is a discussion activity. Make one copy of the worksheet per group of four students. Cut up the sets of cards before the class.

PROCEDURE

1 Review the language for talking about advantages and disadvantages, as well as the language required to build an argument (p80).

2 Students deal out both types of the cards, so that each has the same number.

3 To play a large card, a student must place it in the middle of the group, along with one of the small cards, and describe an advantage or disadvantage of the proposition on the card.

4 The next player must also think of an advantage or disadvantage, share it with the group, and play one of the small cards.

5 When none of the players can think of another advantage or disadvantage to the proposition, the next player can play another large card, with another advantage or disadvantage.

6 The player who finishes using all cards first is the winner.

Notes

Notes

Notes

Notes